The Questions Dictionary of

GEOGRAPHY
& ENVIRONMENT

Joy A Palmer

QUESTIONS
PUBLISHING

THE *QUESTIONS* PUBLISHING COMPANY LTD
BIRMINGHAM
2002

1st Floor, Leonard House,
321 Bradford Street,
Birmingham B5 6ET
Tel: 0121 666 7878
Fax: 0121 666 7879
website: www.education-quest.com

First published in 2001

ISBN: 1 84190 031 1

Designed by Al Stewart
Edited by Diane Parkin
Illustrations by Martin Cater
Cover design by Al Stewart/ Martin Cater

Printed in the UK

To the teacher

The main purpose of this dictionary is to help young people understand the meaning of many of the words they will come across when studying geography and learning about the world around us. Some of the words included relate to describing and explaining aspects of the Earth and its surface. Others explain aspects of life that exist on the Earth, and others relate to the interaction between people and the environment.

The content has been chosen to include words within the capabilities of pupils in the primary and early secondary years of schooling. All words are relevant to the teaching and learning of primary school geography and study of the environment.

The dictionary will make a valuable addition to any primary classroom's collection of basic reference books and to every school's library of geography and environment books. It may be made available for teaching purposes as a book, or as individual word entries, photocopies and fixed to A5 size cards. The book as a whole and its individual entries may be used in a wide variety of ways: by pupils independently or in groups, or together with the teacher. Obviously, individual words or groups of words may be the focus of a particular lesson or line of enquiry, and the dictionary as a whole can be a rich source for browsing through during spare moments.

We emphasise that this book is not simply a list of words and their definitions. Many entries go beyond the straightforward word meaning to provide some explanation, context or example as appropriate – often through the relevant illustrations. Many of the words are linked or related to others and are cross-referenced where appropriate at the head of the entries. Where a word appears in an entry in bold type, this means that it is defined elsewhere in the dictionary. So, if pupils come across a word when studying geography that they are not sure about, or introduced to in a lesson, they can look up what it means and be directed to other relevant words. They can also just pick out any word and be set on a trail of learning of facts and ideas relating to people, other living things and our surroundings. Each entry has a compass symbol above it, indicating which geographical category it comes under. The categories are as follows:

H   Human geography

P   Physical geography

E   Environmental geography

In some cases, the item may fall into more than one category, in which case two or three letters will be shown.

It is hoped that this book will lead both to pupils' better understanding of aspects of our world they may already be familiar with, and to new knowledge and ideas about planet Earth and its life.

Joy A Palmer

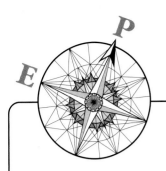

Acid rain

(see also **Weathering**, **pH values**)

Acid rain is the term used to describe **rainfall** and other forms of **precipitation** including snow, sleet, hail and mist which is slightly acid. It has a pH value below five. Acid rain occurs when certain gases emitted from some factories, power stations, chimneys and car exhausts react with water present in the air. Acid rain causes damage to plant life and buildings.

Adaptation

Adaptation means the way living forms gradually change genetically in such ways as to make them better suited to cope with their particular **environmental** conditions. For example, the Arctic fox has become well adapted to its freezing cold **habitat**. It sheds its brown coat in winter and grows a white coat, helping it to be well camouflaged from **predators**.

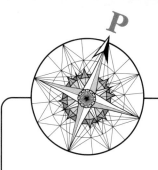

Aerial photograph

An aerial photograph is a picture of a place or **landscape** taken from the air, using an aircraft. Aerial photographs help geographers understand and interpret features of a landscape.

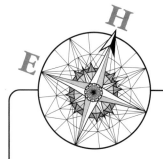

Agenda 21

(see also **United Nations' Conference on Environment and Development**)

Agenda 21 is the name of one of the key documents deriving from the **United Nations' Conference On Environment And Development** held in Rio de Janeiro, Brazil, in 1992. Agenda 21 is a major programme of action designed to bring about **sustainable development** throughout the world. It deals both with the urgent problems facing the planet today and with the need to prepare for the **environmental** challenges of the 21st Century.

Agriculture

Agriculture means the cultivation of **soil** in order to produce crops. Sometimes it is used to mean the production of food in general, that is, pastoral (animal) farming as well as the growing of crops for human or animal consumption.

Agricultural practices vary greatly around the world. In some places simple peasant farmers plant food plants in **forest** clearings or patches of soil near their homes. Elsewhere, agricultural practices involve sophisticated techniques, **technology** and equipment. The type and extent of agriculture in any **locality** depends on skills and technology available, on the **climate** (especially **rainfall** and **temperatures**) and on the type of soil available.

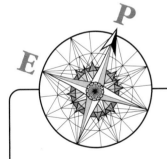

Alternative energy

(see also **Energy**, **Biomass energy** and **Nuclear energy**)

The term alternative energy refers to various methods of producing power or energy, which do not deplete or destroy the **natural resources** of the **Earth**. The technologies used to produce forms of alternative power include solar, **wind**, **tidal** and wave energy, hydroelectricity, geothermal energy (heat from the core of the Earth), and biomass energy.

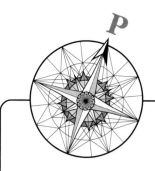

Arid

(see also **Desert** and **Desertification**)

An arid area has very little **rainfall**. The word is usually applied to a **region** of the world or a **climate** in which the rainfall is hardly sufficient to enable **vegetation** to grow. Rainfall in such areas is generally less than 25 mm per year.

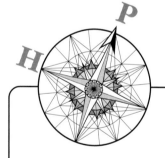

Atlas

(see also **Scale**)

An atlas is a collection of **maps** bound together into a volume or book. A world atlas contains maps of many countries, as well as maps of the whole world. The maps are of different scales.

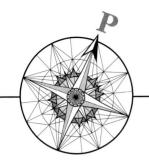

Atmosphere

The atmosphere is one of the three main physical zones of the **Earth**, the others being the **lithosphere** and the **hydrosphere**. The atmosphere consists of the air that we breathe. Without it, there would be no life on Earth. This air is made up of a mixture of gases, mainly Oxygen (21%), Nitrogen (78%), Carbon Dioxide (0.03%), Argon (nearly 1%), Helium and other rare gases (0.1%). With increasing distance from the Earth's surface, the atmosphere becomes more 'rare' or 'thin', i.e. without gases. **Meteorologists** study the amount of water vapour in the atmosphere, which is expressed as 'humidity'.

Atoms

(see also **Radiation** and **Nuclear energy**)

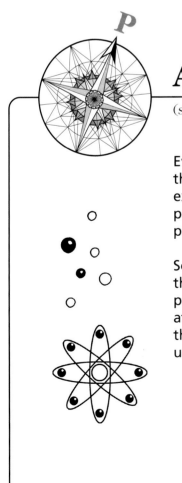

Everything in our world is made up of atoms. Atoms are so small that they are difficult to describe or imagine. One page of this book, for example, is around one million atoms thick. Every atom is made up of particles even tinier than itself. At the centre is a nucleus made up of protons and neutrons. Around the nucleus are one or more electrons.

Some atoms are described as stable. Others are 'unstable'. If there is the correct number of neutrons to balance the number of protons present then the atom is stable. Stable atoms do not change. Unstable atoms have either too many or too few neutrons in the nucleus. When this situation exists, the atoms are radioactive. The nucleus of an unstable atom produces radiation.

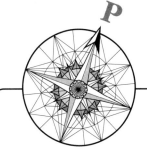

Avalanche

An avalanche is a huge mass of ice and snow which slides down the slope of a **mountain**, carried along by its heavy weight and the pull of gravity. Often avalanches pull very heavy weights of loose **rock** down with them. They are very serious **natural hazards**, which can bury and destroy whole villages, **forests** and roads in their pathway.

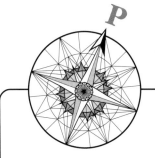

Axis of the Earth

The Axis of the **Earth** is an imaginary line, joining the North Pole and the South Pole, passing through the centre of the **planet**. The Earth rotates on its axis once in every 24 hours.

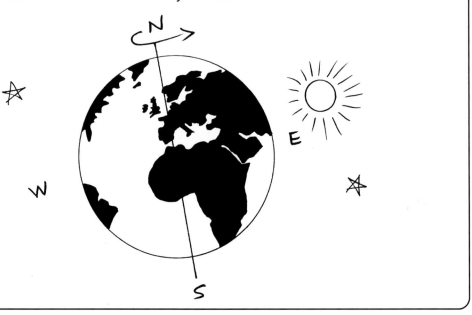

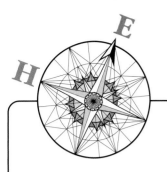

Basic needs

(see also **Rights**)

People's basic needs are fundamental to survival, and include food, water and shelter. Other basic needs include **energy**, sanitation and health care.

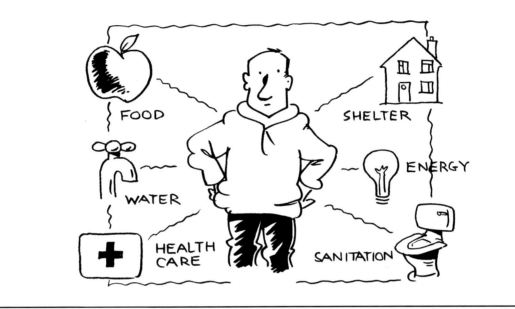

FOOD

SHELTER

WATER

ENERGY

HEALTH CARE

SANITATION

Beaufort scale

Early in the 19th Century a man named Admiral Beaufort devised a scale to differentiate between and describe various strengths of the **wind**. The scale ranges from 0 to 12. 0 represents a calm, almost still air. 12 represents the other extreme, a hurricane wind blowing at over 120 km per hour. The Beaufort Scale uses movement of natural phenomena and objects to describe strengths of wind between 0 and 12. Such descriptions include, for example, drifting smoke, moving leaves and twigs, wind generated waves on water, and violent movement of trees.

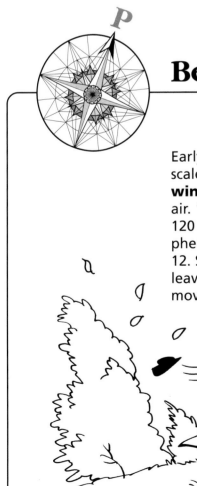

Biodegradable

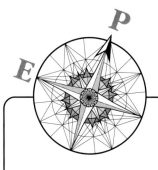

Biodegradable materials are those which decompose or rot down naturally, for example, if they are buried in the ground. Biodegradable objects include leaves and dead insects that rot speedily away and help make rich **fertile soil**. Most plastics and other chemicals are not biodegradable. If they are thrown on to the soil or into water they will stay there and may **pollute** it.

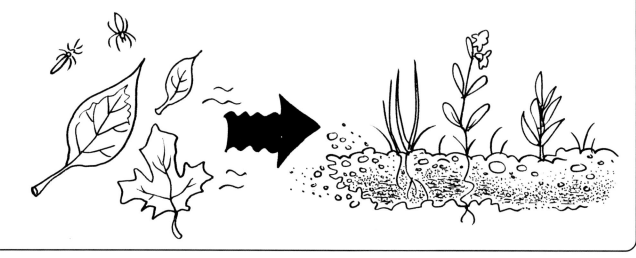

Biodiversity

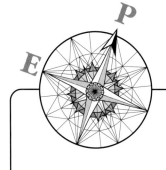

(see also **Tropical rain forests** and **Deforestation**)

Biodiversity refers to the range or **diversity** of plant and animal life. It is the total variety of genetic strains, **species** and ecosystems. Natural ecosystems tend to have a high biodiversity. The impact of people tends to lesson biodiversity, for example, **forest** clearance for **agriculture** reduces biodiversity.

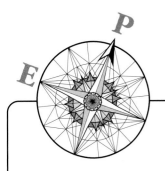

Biomass energy

(see also **Energy** and **Alternative energy**)

Biomass energy is energy derived from living or dead organic matter. In certain parts of the world, notably in **developing** countries, people gather pieces of **wood**, crop **wastes** and animal dung. These materials are dried and burned as fuel. This form of energy production is **sustainable**. It does not use up non-renewable resources.

Biosphere

We live in the biosphere. It is that part of the **Earth** which is occupied by all living things – mammals, birds, fish, reptiles, amphibians, invertebrates, plants, human life and micro-organisms.

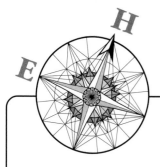

Birth rates

(see also **Population** and **Demography**)

Birth rates are the rates at which human babies are born in a particular location. Usually they are expressed as the number of babies born in a year per thousand of the population. If rates of birth exceed rates of death, then the population of the place is increasing.

Throughout the world, birth rates are higher than death rates and so the number of people on our planet is rising.

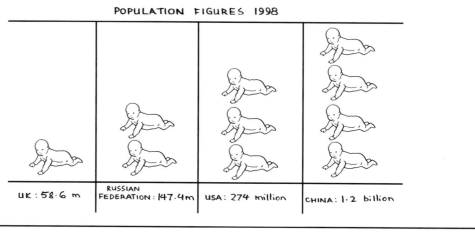

POPULATION FIGURES 1998

| UK : 58·6 m | RUSSIAN FEDERATION : 147·4m | USA : 274 million | CHINA : 1·2 billion |

Bog

A bog is an area of wet, spongy ground. Often bogs form in or around shallow ponds or **lakes**. They consist of decaying or decomposed **vegetation**, such as moss.

Boundary

A boundary is the border between two areas of land which are in some way different or separate. For example, a national boundary marks the limit or extent of the land belonging to a particular country that lies next to another.

Boundaries between countries, **continents** and other defined areas of land are shown on **maps**.

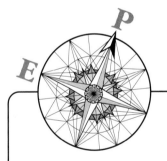

SCOTLAND

ENGLAND

Carrying capacity

The term carrying capacity is used to mean the ability of a particular **environment** or **habitat** to support living things. Every habitat has a limit to the **natural resources** available in it. It can only support so much life without permanent damage to, or destruction of, its resources. If the number of living things increases so much that the place needs more than the resources available, then it has exceeded its carrying capacity. Inevitably then, some things will die.

Cave

A cave is a space that has been hollowed out of the **Earth's** crust below the ground, or out of surface **rocks**. Underground caves are often formed in areas of limestone rock, where **water** containing carbon dioxide dissolves out hollows and passageways. Often a stream runs though caves of this type and **stalactites and stalagmites** may be formed.

Caves at the **coast** are formed by the action of waves lashing against cliffs and causing **erosion** of the rocks.

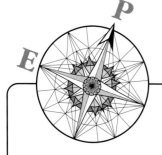

CITES

(see also **Endangered species** and **Protected species**)

The letters CITES stand for the Convention on International Trade in Endangered Species of wild **flora and fauna**. This was established in 1973 and is still the main international mechanism and force for monitoring loss of **species** of animals (fauna) and plants (flora). CITES maintains a list of endangered species which must be protected. In 1992 the African elephant was added to this list, and the sale of ivory was banned.

Citizenship

Citizenship is all about being an informed and responsible citizen, that is, a member of a community or society in general. An informed and responsible citizen has the knowledge, attitudes and skills necessary for making informed decisions about and exercising responsibilities and **rights** in a democratic society.

Climate

(see also **Weather**)

The climate of any particular **region** is the usual or average weather conditions that occur there throughout the **seasons**. Various factors influence climate including the **latitude** of the place, its height above **sea level** and position relative to **mountains** and **oceans**. Certain terms are used to describe the climate in general terms in certain regions. For example, places between the **equator** and the **tropics** of Cancer and Capricorn are said to have a tropical climate. The weather in the tropics is always very hot and there is regular **rainfall**. Other regions have a **temperate** climate, or a Mediterranean climate, and so on.

Clouds

(see also **Rainfall** and **Hydrosphere**)

Clouds consist of masses of tiny droplets of **water** or ice crystals, formed by the condensation of water vapour in the **atmosphere**, high above the **Earth's** surface. **Meteorologists** describe clouds according to their height above the ground. An example of a low cloud (up to 2,500 metres high) is Cumulus. An example of a medium height cloud (2,500 – 5,000 m) is Altostratus. An example of a high cloud (over 5,000 m) is Cirrus. Meteorologists also estimate cloudiness, or the amount of sky covered by cloud at a particular time. The amount of cloud cover is estimated in eighths of sky covered. 0 describes a completely clear sky, 4 describes a sky half covered with clouds and 8 describes a sky entirely covered by clouds.

CIRRUS

CUMULONIMBUS

CUMULUS

ALTOSTRATUS

ALTOCUMULUS

STRATUS

Coast

A coast is the part of the land that borders a sea. It is therefore influenced by **tides** and waves. Many coastlines have beaches made of sand or pebbles that have been deposited on them. Beaches are formed by the tidal action of the sea. Beaches are gradually widened if a cliff standing on the landward side is gradually worn down through **erosion** by the sea's waves constantly lashing against it.

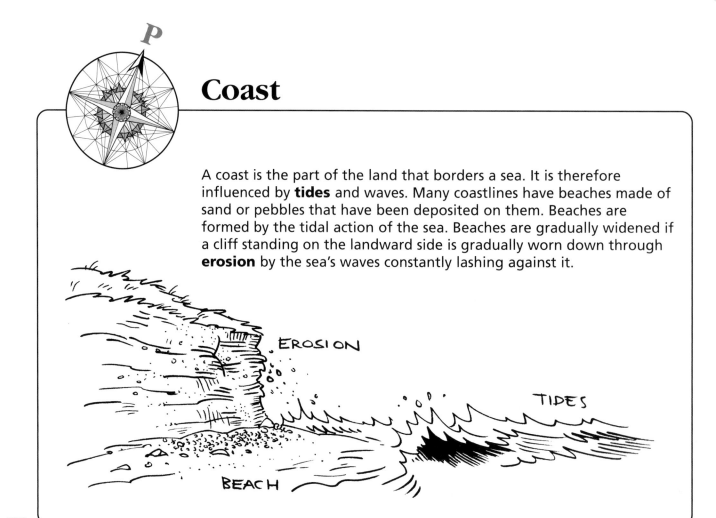

EROSION

TIDES

BEACH

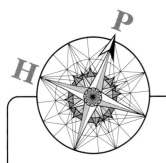

Common land

Common land is land over which a group of people have specified common **rights**. Most frequently, this is the right of common pasture. Much of the hillsides in Wales is common land. In England, the majority of the common land is in the north in areas of moorland and fell.

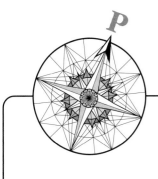

Compass

(see also **North magnetic pole**)

A magnetic compass is an instrument used to measure direction. It contains a magnetised needle, balanced on a fine point, which is free to rotate. The needle swings to a position in which one end points towards the **Earth**'s north magnetic pole. Using other points on the compass it is then possible to tell in which direction you are facing. The four main directions or points of the compass are called the cardinal points. These are north, south, east and west.

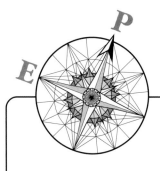

Competition

An **ecologist** uses the word competition to refer to the struggle between individuals or **populations** (of plants or animals) for a limited available resource.

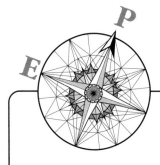

Conservation

Conservation involves protecting and taking care of the world, its life and its resources, so that these things are not damaged or permanently destroyed. Conservation includes such things as protecting animals and plants from becoming **endangered**, protecting the countryside, **forests** and **oceans** from being damaged or **polluted**, taking care not to waste **energy** and disposing of **waste** materials in a responsible manner.

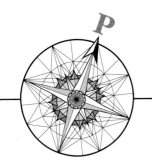

Continents

The **Earth**'s surface is divided into seven large, generally unbroken masses of land, called continents. These are Africa, Antarctica, Asia, Australasia, Europe, North America and South America.

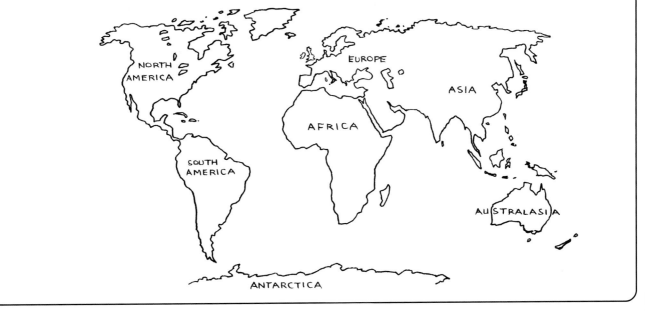

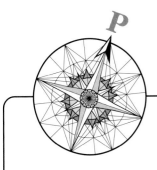

Contour

(see also **Map**, **Sea level** and **Relief**)

A contour is a line drawn on a **map** to join all points which are the same height above **sea level**. A series of contour lines shows the relief of the land of the area covered on a flat map. The intervals between contours may represent relatively small height differences such as 20 metres. On small-scale maps, such as we see in **atlases**, they may represent height differences of hundreds of metres. On **relief maps**, the areas between contours are often shown in different colours. Low land is usually shaded green, and higher land brown. **Mountain** peaks are often shown in white.

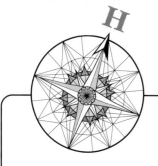

Conurbation

(see also **Urbanisation** and **Settlements**)

A conurbation is a large built up or urban area comprised of buildings, **transportation** networks, businesses, industrial sites and so on. A conurbation develops as neighbouring separate **settlements** grow in size, and eventually expand so much that no open space remains between them. Places that used to have a separate identity become part of the conurbation as a whole. The West Midlands conurbation, for example, is made up of settlements including Birmingham, Solihull, Stourbridge, Walsall, Dudley, Sandwell and Wolverhampton.

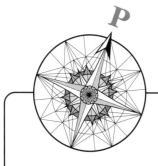

© Questions Publishing Limited

Co-ordinates

Co-ordinate systems provide us with a code for establishing the position of a particular point or place. Co-ordinate systems are used by geographers for interpreting **maps**. In a simple square system we could say that the placed marked ● on this **island** is in the square D8. In a system known as the Cartesian co-ordinate system, the place marked ● is at point coded 8.2. This system can be made even more precise by dividing the numbers into decimal fractions.

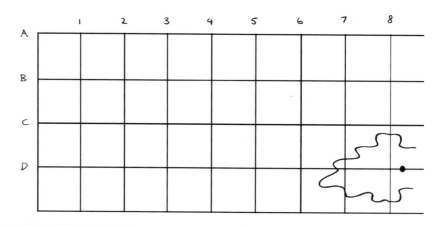

© Questions Publishing Limited

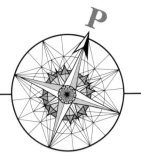

Coral

Coral polyps are small **ocean** creatures with hard skeletons. They can only live in shallow tropical seas. A coral reef is a chain of **rocks** lying on the surface of the sea, which is formed by coral polyps growing together, and fragments of shells and sand.

An atoll is a coral reef in the shape of a ring or horseshoe, which encloses a stretch of water called a lagoon.

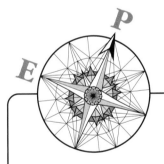

Decomposition

The lives of all plants and animals eventually come to an end. The remains of dead plants and animals, birds and invertebrates rot into the ground and mix with the **soil**, making it richer. This process of rotting or breaking down of dead matter is called decomposition. Decomposed remains provide goodness in the soil that helps new plant life to grow. This process of death leading to new life is called a natural cycle.

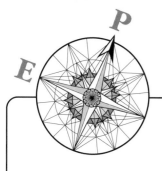

Deforestation

(see also **Tropical rainforests** and **Biodiversity**)

Deforestation is the term used to describe the disappearance of **forests** from large parts of the **Earth**'s surface. The deforestation of tropical rainforests is taking place at an alarming rate. Reasons for deforestation include clearing of trees for the sale of **wood**, and using the land for activities such as cattle ranching, **agriculture**, **mining** and road building.

Degradation

The word degradation may be used to describe the wearing down of the surface of the land, for example, by a **river** which gradually **erodes** the land it passes over and deepens its **valley**. Degradation is also used more generally to describe any form of destruction, spoiling or reducing the quality of a **landscape** or the **environment**. Environmental degradation is a major concern in the world today. In many places, human activity is resulting in irreparable damage to the natural world. This is the case in developed, **industrialised** countries and also in the **developing world** where people often contribute to the further degradation of already poor environments as they work for survival.

Delta

A delta is a fan-shaped area that exists at the mouth of some of the world's **rivers**. Sometimes, as a **river** flows into the sea, it deposits more solid material or **sediment**, on to the ground than can be washed away by the **tides**. So an area of land develops. As more material is deposited, the **river** divides and flows to each side of it, forming new banks and channels. As this process continues over many years, a whole network of divisions and water channels is created, with areas of flat wet land between them. In many of the great delta areas of the world, people live on and cultivate the land between the watercourses. Well known deltas include the Amazon, the Nile, the Mississippi, the Ganges and the Danube.

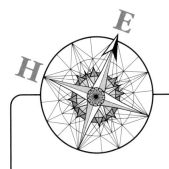

Demography

The term demography means the study of **populations**. It is the statistical analysis of births, deaths, **migrations** and disease, and their influence on numbers of people. It helps geographers know about the conditions of life in countries or communities. Demographic means relating to demography. A demographic transition is a pattern of changes in which **birth rates** fall as, or after, death rates fall. After such a transition, a country's birth rate is closer to its death rate and so the population does not grow rapidly.

WORLD POPULATION

Desert

(see also **Arid**, **Desertification** and **Tundra**)

A desert is an area of land with an **arid climate**. **Precipitation** is so light or spasmodic that very little **vegetation** can grow. The surface of a desert may be comprised of **rocks**, stones or sand. Many of the world's hot deserts are in **tropical** areas. These include the Sahara and the Arabian Deserts. Other deserts are in mid-**latitude** areas. Not all deserts are hot. In some high latitude or high altitude places, vegetation cannot grow because of lack of precipitation and low **temperatures**. Such barren tracts of land are called cold deserts, or **tundra**.

HOT   COLD

Desertification

(see also **Arid** and **Desert**)

Desertification is the process in which good **soils** are reduced to **deserts** as a result of human interference or actions and changing **climates**. It describes the destruction and exhaustion of soils around the world. **Fertile** lands are being reduced to deserts through over-grazing, over-cultivation, the destruction of **forests** and poor **irrigation**.

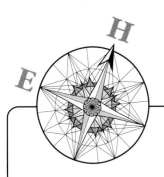

Developing world

(see also **Degradation**, **Basic needs** and **Development**)

In countries of the so-called developing world, large proportions of the **population** live in physical **environments** in which securing basic needs is very difficult. Such environments are likely to be detrimental to **health**. Common characteristics of **settlements** in developing countries include rapid population growth, severe **poverty**, high levels of unemployment, inadequate housing, lack of skilled or trained people, widespread poor health and increasing **urbanisation**. Many developing countries are in the world's **tropical regions**.

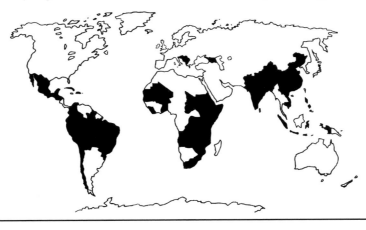

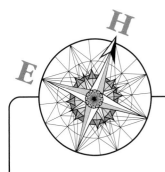

Development

(see also **Sustainable development** and **Developing world**)

The process of development of societies involves making progress or changes in them, which seem to be for the better. Development should enable people to have a better standard of living and quality of life. It encompasses economic and social issues and activities; also the use of **natural resources**. Inevitably, development and the greater use of resources have resulting impacts upon the **environment**.

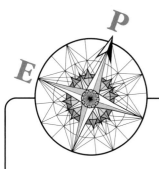

Diversity

(see also **biodiversity**)

The term diversity as used by geographers and **environmentalists** refers to the variety, or differences in kind that exist among **species**, ecosystems or ways of life.

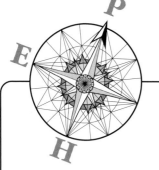

Earth

(see also **Solar system**, **Lithosphere** and **Atmosphere**)

The Earth is one of the major planets of the **solar system**. It is the fifth largest in size and the third in terms of distance from the **Sun**. The Earth has a solid outer crust or **lithosphere** and is surrounded by a layer of air called the **atmosphere**. As far as we know, the Earth is the only planet in the **solar system** that supports human life.

Geography is the subject that describes and explains the **Earth**'s surface and aspects of life which exist on it, and the interaction between people and the **environment**.

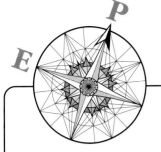

Earthquake

(see also **Natural hazards**)

An earthquake is a movement or tremor of the crust of the **Earth**. The tremor begins below the surface, but can sometimes cause shaking or movement at the surface of the ground itself. In a severe earthquake, the ground surface may actually develop cracks as changes to its level or position occur. Earthquakes may cause buildings to sway backwards and forwards, or even collapse completely. Indeed a great deal of damage can be caused by earthquakes. They may even destroy whole cities.

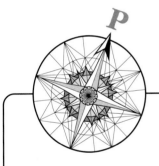

Eclipse

During an eclipse of the **Sun**, the Sun's light is obscured by the Moon, which is passing between the **Earth** and the Sun, casting a shadow on the Earth. If the Sun is completely obscured, it is called a total solar eclipse. If the Sun's light is only partly obscured it is called a partial solar eclipse. During a lunar eclipse, the light of the Moon is obscured by the Earth, which is passing between the Sun and the Moon, casting a shadow on the Moon. If the Moon is completely obscured it is called a total lunar eclipse. If the Moon is only partly obscured, it is called a partial lunar eclipse.

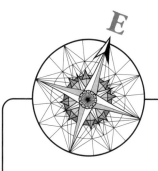

Eco-labelling

Eco-labelling refers to the labelling of manufactured products or **retail** goods to indicate that they have satisfied certain conditions of significance to the **environment**. Eco-labelling identifies environmentally friendly items that have been manufactured without damage to the environment or depletion of **non-renewable resources**.

Ecology

Ecology is the study of the relationships among plants and animals and the **environment** in which they live. Ecologists are interested in how all forms of life interact with each other, and how their numbers are limited by the resources available to them.

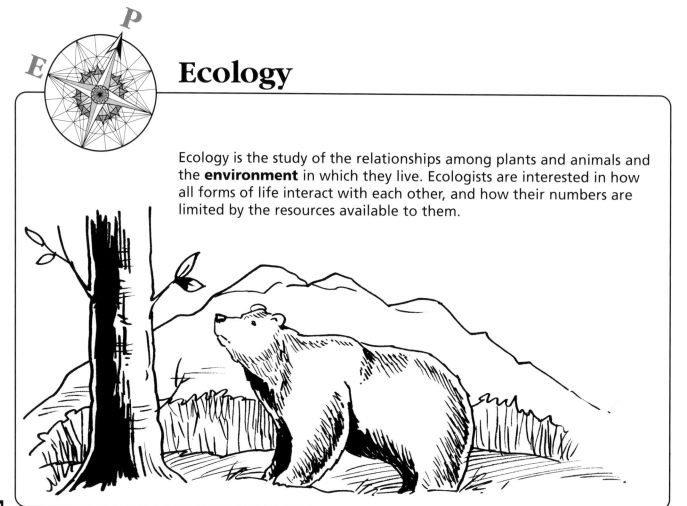

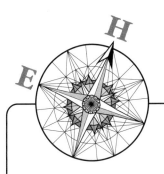

Economics

Economics means the management of finances or monetary matters. It is the branch of knowledge that deals with the production and distribution of wealth in both theory and practice.

Eco-tourism

(see also **Leisure**)

Eco-tourism is tourism that is planned to take care of and protect the **environment**, rather than damage, destroy or pollute it.

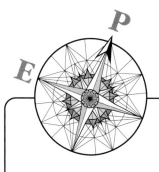

Endangered species

(see also **Cites** and **Protected species**)

Many **wildlife** species face an increasing number of threats to their survival as a result of direct or indirect interference by people. Some species have died out altogether (become extinct) because their **habitats** have been destroyed or because they themselves have been hunted or harmed. Animal species which are dying out in large numbers or which are likely to do so are called endangered species.

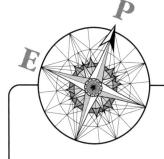

Energy

(see also **Alternative energy**, **Biomass energy** and **Nuclear energy**)

Energy is the power by which anything acts to move or change things. Energy is all around us and it makes things happen. Nothing could move without energy in some form or another, and there are many different kinds of energy. The **Sun**'s energy is the basis of life on **Earth**. Without sunlight, there would be no plant life. Without plants there would be no animals and, without plants and animals, no people. Energy can be stored and made available in various ways. Food is a form of energy; so are fuels such as gas, coal, oil and **wood**.

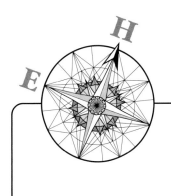

Environment

(see also **Habitat**)

The environment is our surroundings on **Earth**. All life on the planet depends on the environment for its survival. The environment includes land, water and air.

Often the word is used in this very general way, to describe our surroundings. It may also be used to describe a particular place or habitat, for example, a city environment, a **coastal** environment, and so on.

Environmentalist

(see also **Green**)

An environmentalist is a person who shows concern about or takes action to protect the **environment**. Environmentalists may engage in such things as **recycling** their **waste**, buying goods made from **renewable resources** and walking or cycling rather than driving vehicles, which **pollute** the air.

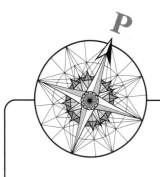

Equator

(see also **Hemisphere**)

The equator is an imaginary circular line running around the centre of the **Earth**. It is midway between the North and South Poles.

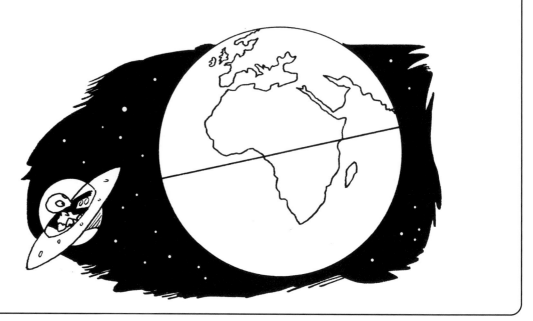

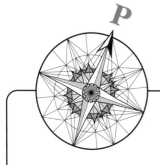

Erosion

Erosion is the term used to describe the wearing away of the surface of the land by natural means. **Water** on the move in the form of **rivers**, **rainfall** and the waves of the sea constantly wears away or erodes the land it washes against. **Glaciers**, ice, frost, **wind** and melting snow are other examples of natural agents of erosion. The shapes of **landscapes** and **landforms** may alter considerably over a long period of time as a result of natural erosion.

European Union

The European Union is an association of countries in the **continent** of **Europe**. The six original members – Belgium, France, West Germany, Italy, Luxembourg and the Netherlands – were joined by the UK, Denmark and the Republic of Ireland in 1973, Greece in 1981, Spain and Portugal in 1986, East Germany in 1990 (on reunification of Germany), and Austria, Finland and Sweden in 1995. Other countries await full membership. Aims of the European Union include the expansion of **trade**, the encouragement of free movement of capital and **human resources** within the association, and the creation of a closer union or community among the people of Europe.

Evolution

Evolution is the process by which **species** have changed and developed to their present appearance and genetic form. The process of evolution involves natural selection, which means that as time goes by, those individuals best suited to their **environment** are most likely to survive.

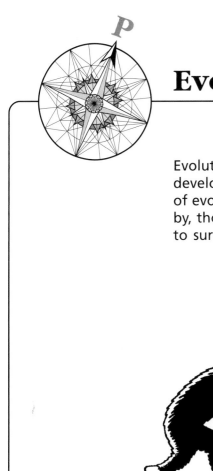

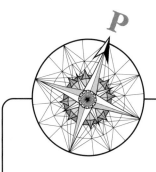

Fertile

(see also **Organic fertilisers**)

Fertile is a word used to describe **soil** that is rich in the materials needed to support **vegetation**. If soil is not sufficiently rich, then farmers may apply substances called **fertiliser** to the soil, which help to support plant growth.

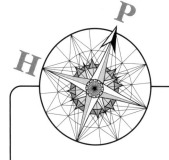

Flight

Many things are capable of flight, that is, moving through the air. Some of these are natural fliers from the world of animals, birds and insects, while others are man-made craft, powered to fly by a variety of sources. Modern aircraft are powered by jet engines.

Flight is important to our world for a variety of reasons. It gives people pleasure and has many practical uses such as international travel and **trade**.

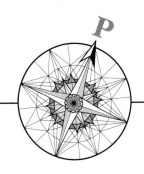

Floods

(see also **Natural hazards**)

A **river** is said to flood when its **water** level rises and it overflows its banks. Some rivers flood regularly and are bordered by areas of flat marshy ground called flood plains.

Unexpected floods can be serious natural hazards. Very high floodwater may enter riverside towns and villages causing a lot of damage and threat to life.

If **sea level** rises, **coastal** land and **settlements** may be flooded. Scientists are worried that **global warming** may lead to rising sea levels and subsequent flooding of land.

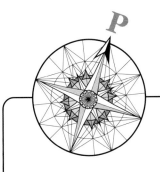

Flora and fauna

Flora and fauna is a phrase used by **ecologists** and other scientists for plants (flora) and animals (fauna) that may be found in a given area at a particular time.

FLORA   FAUNA

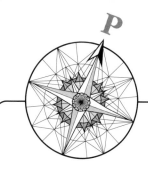

Food chains

Animals, including birds and fish, depend on plants and animals for food. These relationships of **interdependence** for survival involve food chains, or essential links between 'who eats who' or 'who eats what'. A **species** may become **endangered** or extinct if key members of a food chain are missing.

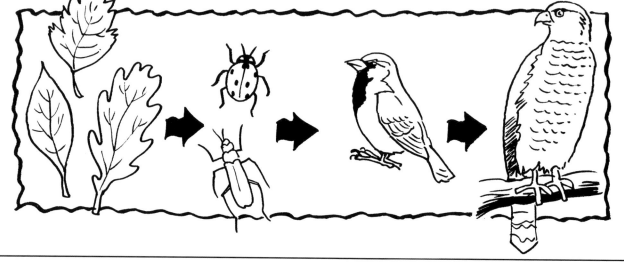

© Questions Publishing Limited

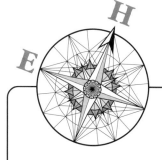

Foreign aid

(see also **World Bank**)

Foreign aid is money dedicated to the **developing world** by a foreign donor. Aid may be given as a grant or a loan. The purpose is to transfer resources from already wealthy (developed) countries to poor nations so that they might be assisted with **development**. Donors may be banks, governments or other agencies or organisations. If foreign aid is to be successful, it is essential that it is used for environmentally **sustainable** projects and not projects that cause **degradation**.

© Questions Publishing Limited

Forests

(see also **Tropical rainforests** and **Deforestation**)

A forest is an extensive area of land that is covered with trees. Some forests are naturally growing. Others have been planted by people. It is possible to describe various types of forest according to the type of trees growing, or their location in the world. For example, a coniferous forest is a forest of evergreen coniferous (cone bearing) trees. **Wood** from these trees is described as softwood and has many uses. A deciduous forest is comprised of broadleaf trees that lose their leaves for part of the year. The valuable wood from deciduous forests is 'hardwood', which is very strong and hard wearing.

SOFTWOODS   HARDWOODS

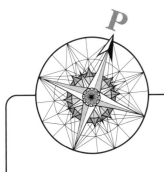

Fossil

(see also **Fossil fuels**)

Fossils are the remains of plants and animals that have been buried and preserved in the **rocks** of the **Earth** for an extremely long time. They are evidence of life in the past.

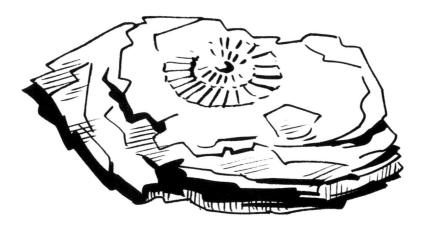

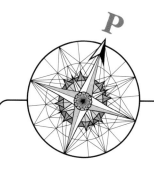

Fossil fuels

(see also **Fossil**)

Fossil fuels are fuels that are derived from the **Earth's rocks**, notably coal, natural gas and peat.

Coal seams often contain fossilised remains of the plants which formed them.

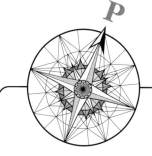

Fresh water

(see also **Wetlands**)

The term fresh water is used to describe all of the water on our **Earth** that is not salty. In other words, it refers to sources of water other than the **Oceans**, which are composed of salty water.

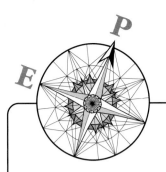

Gaia

Gaia is the name of the Goddess Earth in Greek mythology. It is used by some scientists for the idea that the whole **Earth**, like a healthy human body, functions as a single organism which defines and maintains the conditions necessary for its survival.

Genetic engineering

Genetic engineering refers to the practice of changing the nature or properties of a living organism through adding, removing or copying genes. Genes are the parts of a cell that transmit particular characteristics from a parent to an offspring.

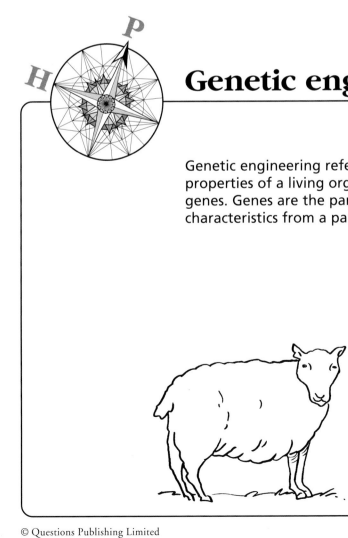
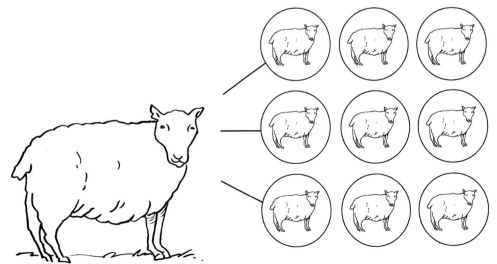

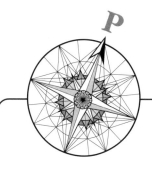

Glacier

A glacier is a mass of ice, which moves slowly down a **valley** under the force of gravity. Usually a glacier originates above the snowline of a **mountain** above which there is always snow on the ground. A glacier is likely to extend far below the snowline. Glaciers are usually tongue-shaped. They are broadest near to the source and at their narrowest where they finish. The movement of glaciers causes **erosion** of the land's surface and the shaping of valleys.

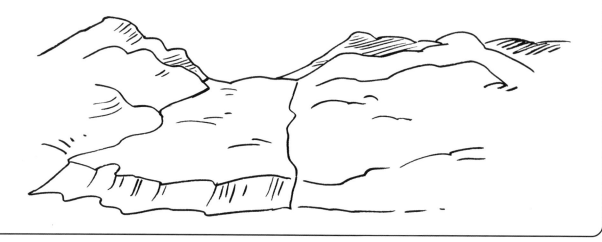

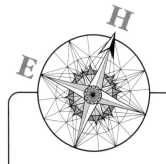

Global commons

Global commons is a term used by **environmentalists** to refer to those parts of the planet which do not belong to, and are not managed by, any one country or group of countries in particular. Global commons, or the world's shared areas, include the **oceans**, outer space and Antarctica.

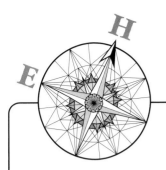

Global village

Global village is a term used by people who consider that our world is a single community, brought together by modern high **technology** and sophisticated forms of international communication (such as the Internet).

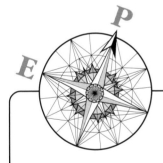

Global warming

(see also **Greenhouse effect, Floods** and **Ozone layer**)

Global warming means an increase in **temperature** at the surface of the **Earth**, supposedly caused by the **greenhouse effect**. If too much heat is retained in the **atmosphere**, and not enough escapes, the **air** will become warmer and various changes in the climate of the Earth will take place. Scientists are very concerned about the possible consequences of global warming. If the **climate** of **polar** lands change and ice melts, **sea levels** would rise and **floods** would occur. This is one of many potentially very serious consequences.

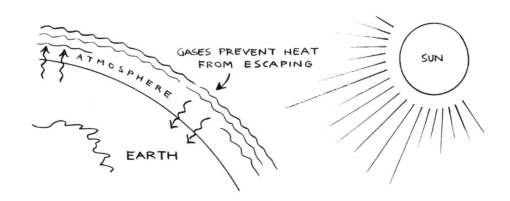

GASES PREVENT HEAT FROM ESCAPING

ATMOSPHERE

SUN

EARTH

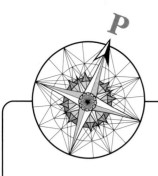

Globe

The word globe means a spherical body. We use it to describe the shape of the **Earth**. A spherical model, showing the **continents** and **oceans** of the whole Earth's surface is also called a globe.

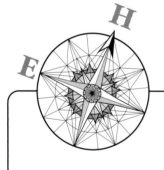

Green

(see also **Environmentalist**)

A green person is someone who is a supporter of environmentalism. A green person is a **conservationist**, who takes action to protect the **environment**, and who may be a member of an ecological political party.

Greenhouse effect

(see also **Global warming**)

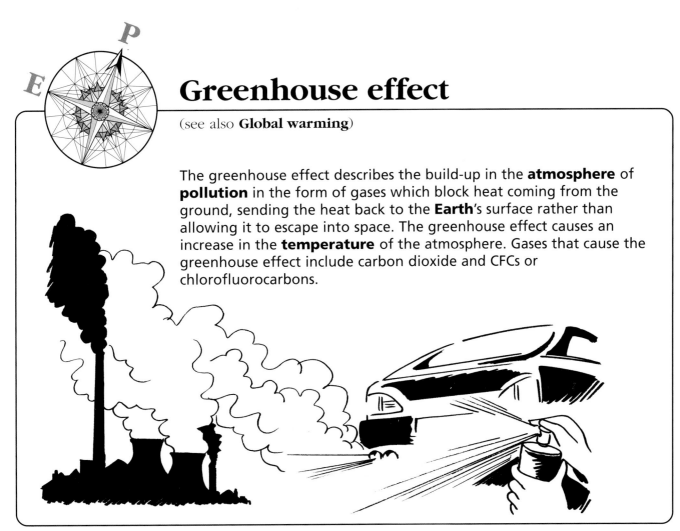

The greenhouse effect describes the build-up in the **atmosphere** of **pollution** in the form of gases which block heat coming from the ground, sending the heat back to the **Earth**'s surface rather than allowing it to escape into space. The greenhouse effect causes an increase in the **temperature** of the atmosphere. Gases that cause the greenhouse effect include carbon dioxide and CFCs or chlorofluorocarbons.

Greenwich Mean Time (GMT)

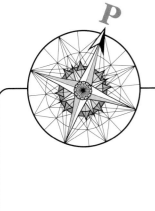

Greenwich Mean Time, or GMT, is the Standard Time in the British Isles. It is the local time at Greenwich in London. This time is also used as a standard time for calculating differences between GMT and the local time in other countries in the world. Nearby countries in Europe such as France and Spain are one hour ahead of GMT. When it is 08.00 GMT, it is 09.00 in Paris. The time difference is greater elsewhere and varies according to direction and distance from London. For example, New York, USA is five hours behind GMT. San Francisco, USA is eight hours behind GMT. Sydney, Australia is ten hours ahead of GMT.

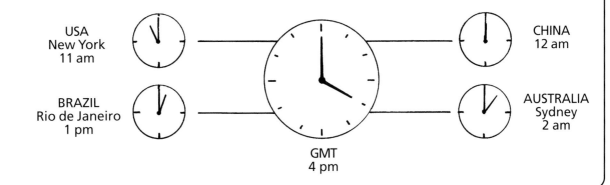

USA New York 11 am

BRAZIL Rio de Janeiro 1 pm

GMT 4 pm

CHINA 12 am

AUSTRALIA Sydney 2 am

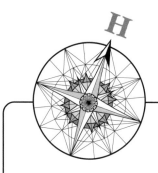

Gross Domestic Product (GDP)

The Gross Domestic Product is the annual total value of goods produced and services provided in any particular country. The GDP does not include the funds gained from transactions or **trade** with other countries.

Growing season

In any **region** of the world, natural **vegetation** has a growing season. This **season** consists of the months or part of every year when the local **climate** enables the vegetation to grow. **Rainfall** and **temperatures** influence every **locality**'s growing season. In the **tundra**, this season lasts only for about two months. In other places, such as **tropical rain forests**, the growing season goes on all through the year.

The growing season of a regioninevitably affects its **agriculture**. For example, certain crops may not grow in a time of year with too little rainfall unless it is possible to provide **irrigation**.

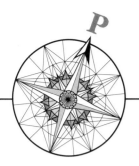

Habitat

A habitat is the natural home of animals and plants. The word may be applied to locations on a variety of scales, for example a single tree, a meadow or a whole **forest**.

FOREST

TREE

OCEAN

HILLS

RIVER

MEADOW

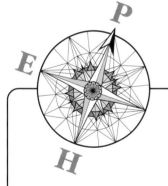

Hazardous waste

(see also **Waste** and **Landfill**)

Hazardous waste is waste that will cause damage to the **environment** and human **health** if it is placed in landfills, the air or **water** in a raw or untreated form. Hazardous waste includes **nuclear** materials, toxic materials (e.g. chemicals from **industrial** processes), flammables (things that will easily burn), explosives and carcinogenics (things that are known to cause cancer). There is major **trade** in hazardous waste. Every year, many tonnes of it are **exported** from industrialised countries to the **developing world**.

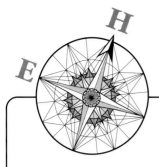

Health and environment

(see also **Developing world**)

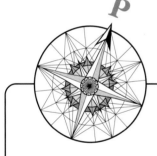

The nature and quality of the **environment** in which people live and lifestyles within that environment have a major impact upon human health and well-being. In developed countries levels of income, as expressed by social class, are closely related to premature deaths. In the **developing world**, healthy environments are characterised by the provision of health care, supplies of clean water, good sanitation facilities, safe housing and the absence of air **pollution**. Yet many people in developing countries live in extremely unhealthy environments. Around four million children die every year of diarrhoeal diseases resulting from poor water quality and lack of sanitation. Many millions of people are malnourished and hence very likely to die of various diseases.

Hemisphere

A hemisphere is half of the surface of the **Earth**. The Northern Hemisphere is the half of the Earth that lies north of the **equator**. The Southern Hemisphere is the half which lies south of the equator.

Heritage

Heritage is that which is or may be inherited; that is, passed on from one generation to another. Some places in the world are considered so special that they are deemed to be heritage sites. They are places of particular beauty or cultural or historical importance and are protected from **development** or change. This means that people in one generation cannot alter or destroy such sites so that succeeding generations cannot enjoy or appreciate them.

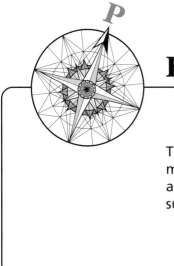

Horizon

The word horizon describes the apparent line of where **Earth** and sky meet as you look into the far distance. The horizon is easy to see if you are on a beach looking out to sea. On land, the horizon is broken up by such things as hills and buildings.

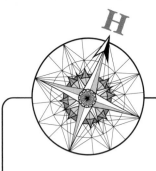

Human resources

Human resources are the people, especially employees (workers and other personnel), who are regarded as an asset in a business or organisation.

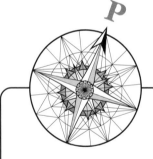

Hydrosphere

(see also **Precipitation** and **Rainfall**)

The hydrosphere is one of the three main physical zones of the **Earth**, the others being the **atmosphere** and the **lithosphere**. The hydrosphere consists of the **water** that covers around 70% of the Earth's surface in the form of **oceans**, **seas** and **lakes**.

Water evaporates from the surface of water on the Earth and rises as water vapour into the air. High up in the atmosphere, water vapour condenses and forms **clouds**. From the clouds, **precipitation** falls back to Earth. This constant process of evaporation, condensation and precipitation is known as the hydrological or water cycle.

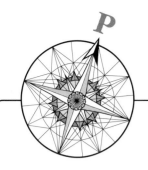

Ice age

An ice age is a period of time when **glaciers** and sheets of ice cover large areas of the world's **continents**. The most recent major ice age began about two million years ago. During this ice age, ice covered much of Europe and North America. Today ice sheets remaining from this time still exist in the Antarctic and Greenland.

Iceberg

An iceberg is a mass of ice that has come adrift from a **glacier** or ice sheet and is floating in the sea. Icebergs are commonly found in the waters near Antarctica and Greenland. They may protrude to a height of around 100 metres above the sea and be up to 70 kilometres in length. The extent of an iceberg below the surface is always far greater than the visible part of it. Because a good deal of it is hidden in the water, an iceberg can be very dangerous for ships passing nearby.

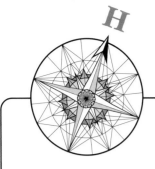

Imports and exports

(see also **Trade**)

Imports are items or goods that are brought into a country from elsewhere. Goods may be imported because a country finds them difficult or impossible to produce itself, or because it is cheaper to buy them from elsewhere than to produce them at home. Sometimes available land and labour are better used for other purposes, perhaps to produce something that a country is particularly well placed to produce. Goods produced within a country, which are sold in trade elsewhere, are known as exports. Exports may be thought of as goods exchanged for imports.

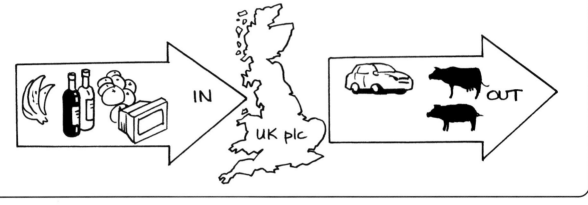

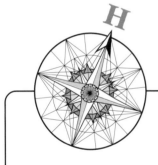

Indigenous people

Indigenous people are those who are native to a particular **region**; that is, they belong naturally there. They, and their ancestors were born in the place in question, and their ancestors were the original inhabitants of their lands. Indigenous people include the Aborigines of Australia, the Maoris of New Zealand, and Indians of North and South America.

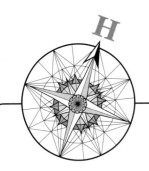

Industry and industrialisation

(see also **Raw materials** and **Renewable resources**)

The word industry is often associated with factories: places where large numbers of identical articles are made by the use of machines. Some of Britain's big cities, such as Birmingham, Manchester and Leeds, developed during a period known as the Industrial Revolution, a time of very rapid **development**of the nation's industry through the introduction of machines. Many industries use raw materials to produce goods needed by society. Not all industry is carried out in large factories. Small businesses may be started in people's homes or small workshops. Industrialisation is the process of becoming industrial or developing industries.

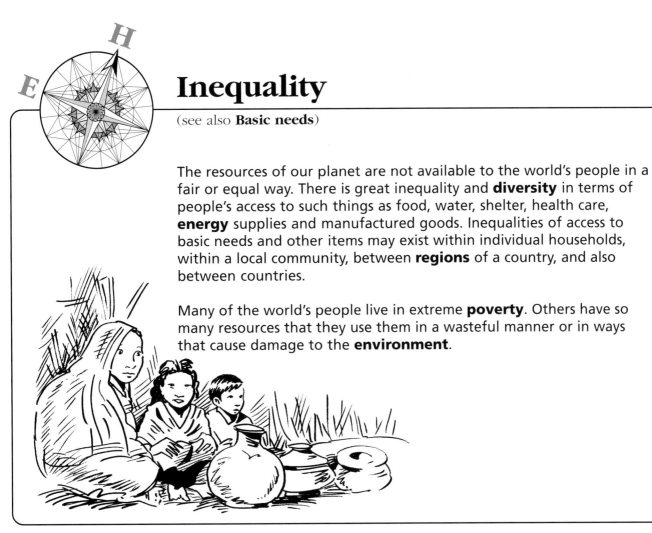

Inequality

(see also **Basic needs**)

The resources of our planet are not available to the world's people in a fair or equal way. There is great inequality and **diversity** in terms of people's access to such things as food, water, shelter, health care, **energy** supplies and manufactured goods. Inequalities of access to basic needs and other items may exist within individual households, within a local community, between **regions** of a country, and also between countries.

Many of the world's people live in extreme **poverty**. Others have so many resources that they use them in a wasteful manner or in ways that cause damage to the **environment**.

Interdependence

(see also **Food chains** and **Decomposition**)

Plants, animals, and human life depend upon each other for survival. Plants grow in **soil** enriched by decomposition of other living things. Animals and humans depend upon plants and other animals (including fish and birds) for food. They are linked together in food chains.

The world's people and places are also linked interdependently. Issues such as **energy**, employment, **trade**, travel and communications are all linked within the overall world economy.

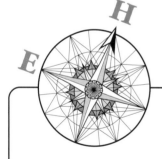

International co-operation

International co-operation means the coming together of two or more countries in an agreement to act in a particular way or achieve certain goals. **Agenda 21** makes it clear that **sustainable development** is primarily the responsibility of governments around the world. It can only be achieved with both national strategies, **plans** and policies, and also with a good deal of international co-operation and agreed plans for action at a global level.

Irrigation

Irrigation is a term used to describe the process of distributing **water** on land artificially. Irrigating techniques are used to enable crops to grow in places where they would otherwise be unable to because of lack of sufficient water. People in many places in the world would not be able to engage in **agriculture** without means of irrigation. Some methods are very simple indeed, for example, pulling water by hand from a **well**. In other locations, modern **technology** is used to control complex systems of watering the land.

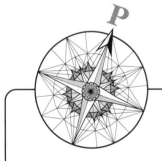

Island

An island is a piece of land surrounded by **water**. Islands may be situated in an **ocean**, sea, **lake** or **river**. Islands are formed in a wide variety of ways. Some are created when sand, **soil** or sediment is deposited along the seashore or in a river. Others are formed by deposits of **coral**, by movement of the crust of the **Earth**, by the rising of the ocean bed, the falling of the level of the sea, by the tips of **volcanoes** which protrude above the sea's surface, or by the sinking of areas of **coastal** land.

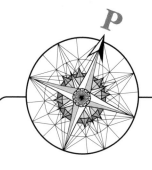

Key

(see also **Symbols**)

A key on a **map** or **plan** is the explanation of the symbols that are used to show features in two-dimensional form.

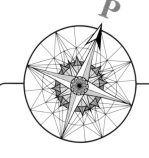

Lake

A lake is an expanse of **water**, surrounded by land, which occupies a hollow in the surface of the **Earth**. **Rivers** may flow in and out of lakes. Water will be lost from a lake through the process of evaporation. Usually the amount of water entering a lake is greater than that lost and so a stream of water will flow out. However, in **arid** lands and places where **rainfall** varies greatly from **season** to season, the level of lakes will vary considerably throughout the year. Lakes may dry out completely in hot, dry periods.

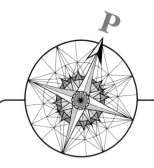

Landfill sites

(see also **Waste**)

Landfill sites are places where waste materials are disposed of by burying them under layers of **soil**, filling up a huge hole in the ground. Usually, waste materials that are not **recycled** are either incinerated or disposed of in landfills.

© Questions Publishing Limited

Landform

Landform is a term used by geographers to describe a particular physical feature on the **Earth**'s surface, for example, a hill, a **plateau**, or a cliff.

© Questions Publishing Limited

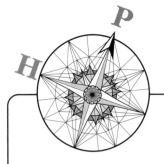

Landscape

The landscape is the natural scenery we see around us when looking out over a particular view or place. A landscape painter is an artist who paints landscapes; a landscape architect **plans** and designs open air **environments**.

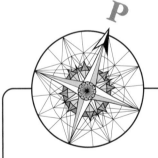

Latitude and longitude

(see also **Equator** and **Greenwich Mean Time**)

Latitudes tell us how far south or north a place is. Lines of latitude are imaginary lines on the surface of the world, parallel to the equator. They measure degrees north or south of the equator.

Longitudes tell us how far west or east a place is. They are also known as meridians and cross the **globe** vertically from North Pole to South Pole. Degrees east and west are measured from Greenwich, the 'Prime Meridian'.

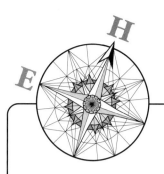

Leisure

(see also **Eco-tourism**)

Our leisure is the time when we are not working. Many activities can occupy our leisure. Some activities such as sports need us to be active, and others, such as watching TV, help us to rest.

Often we associate leisure with holidays and going out and about. Leisure activities can sometimes cause damage to the **environment** and **pollution** of land, air and water.

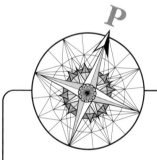

Lithosphere

(see also **Continents**)

The lithosphere is one of the three main physical zones of the **Earth**, the others being the **atmosphere** and the **hydrosphere**. The lithosphere comprises the Earth's solid crust. It consists of the loose layer known as **soil** and the mass of hard **rock** of the Earth beneath this, which is many kilometres deep. The lithosphere appears above the hydrosphere and forms the world's landmasses or continents.

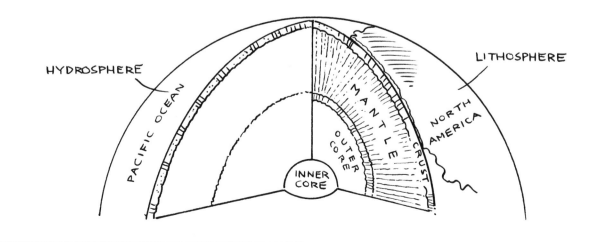

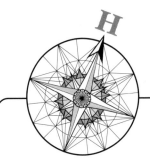

Locality

(see also **Region**)

The locality means the local area; the features or surroundings of a particular place. The word is also used to describe an area or district with particular local characteristics or people. People often regard their own locality as a particular 'spot' or place they belong to and feel at home in.

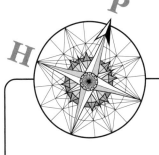

Map

(see also **Ordnance survey**, **Relief**, **Plan** and **Scale**)

A map shows a representation of all or part of the curved surface of the **Earth** on a flat surface. Each point on the map corresponds to an actual position according to a definite scale. Maps may be designed to show a wide variety of features, for example: roads and buildings in a town; **settlements** in a particular **locality**; physical features such as **mountains**, **rivers** and **valleys**; relief of the land; footpaths through the countryside; and the countries of the world.

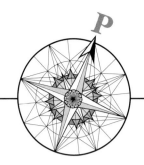

Meteorology

(see also **Atmosphere** and **Weather**)

Meteorology is the science that investigates and reports on the weather. Meteorologists study the physical processes taking place in the atmosphere, and related processes taking place in the **hydrosphere** and **lithosphere**. Meteorologists investigate pressure, **winds**, **clouds**, sunshine and **precipitation**.

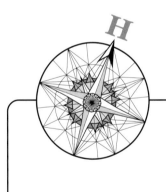

Migration

Migration is the term used to describe the temporary movement of living things from one place to another. Certain **species** of animals and birds migrate regularly, in order to move to a warmer or more suitable **climate** for some months of each year. Some people, for example, peasant farmers in certain locations, also migrate. They change their abode with the **seasons** in order to maximise their potential to farm the land.

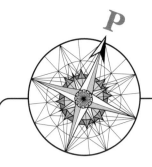

Minerals

(see also **Raw materials** and **Industry**)

Minerals are natural substances that are extracted from the **Earth** by **mining**. Some minerals, for example coal, are organic. Coal consists of carbonised vegetable matter. Many minerals are not organic (that is, not made of animal or vegetable matter). Unlike **rock**, inorganic minerals have a definite chemical composition and have physical and chemical properties.

There are about 2,000 known minerals in the world. Some minerals make beautiful shapes called crystals. Examples of minerals include nickel, copper, aluminium, salt, mercury, zinc and lead. Minerals are widely used as raw materials in industry. They are also essential in other aspects of our lives including **agriculture**, medicine and the production of **energy**.

SALT   SULPHUR   QUARTZ

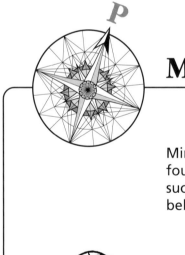

Mining

Mining is the process of excavation for the extraction of materials found deep down in the **Earth**'s crust. Mines are constructed to remove such things as coal, metal, metallic ores, salt and other **minerals** from below ground and bring them to the surface for use.

COAL MINE   OPENCAST MINE

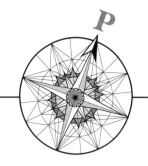

Monsoon

A monsoon is a seasonal **wind** which prevails in Southern Asia, and which reverses its direction from **season** to season. In the heat of the summer, the south-west monsoon blows, bringing torrential rain. In winter, the north-east monsoon blows, which is a cold, dry wind.

Mountains

Mountains are masses of land which are very much higher than the neighbouring **landscape**. Mountains are higher than hills, though there is no agreed height at which a feature becomes known as a mountain. The summit area or peak of a mountain is small in proportion to the area of its base. Most of the world's highest mountains do not occur as single peaks. They are arranged in groups or ranges. Mountains are formed in a variety of ways, including movements of the **Earth**'s surface, **erosion** of softer **rocks** and the action of **volcanoes**.

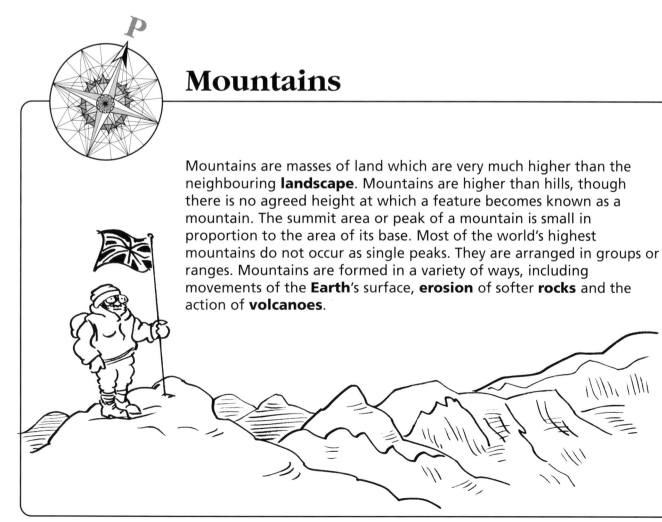

Natural hazards

(see also **Avalanche**, **Earthquake**, **Floods** and **Volcano**)

Natural hazards are dangers that exist in our world which people have no control over and which have the potential for causing disasters. Natural hazards include avalanches, earthquakes, **hurricanes**, **tornadoes** and volcanoes. Such hazards of the physical **environment** can cause large-scale loss of life, serious injury and destruction of **settlements** and **resources**. People who dwell in places where such disasters are most likely to occur live with added risk in their lives.

Natural resources

(see also **Renewable resources**)

Natural resources are the **Earth**'s sources of **raw materials** or **energy**. They include such things as timber, coal, oil, gas, water, iron and aluminium.

Some of the world's presently available resources are renewable. Others are not and have the potential to be used up completely unless they are used sustainably.

COAL

OIL

TIMBER

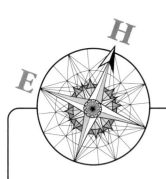

NGOs

A non-governmental organisation (NGO) is an organisation that does not belong to and is not associated with a government. Many NGOs are involved in **environmental**, **conservation** and **green** issues. They play a key role in working alongside the world's governments, businesses and individuals in efforts to promote environmental awareness, protection and **sustainable devleopment**. Examples of NGOs include the World Wide Fund for Nature (WWF) and Oxfam.

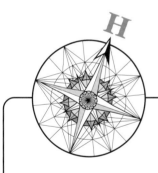

Nomads

Nomads are people who regularly change their place of living. For example, in the **steppes** and some **desert** areas, nomads stay in one place for part of the year, notably during the **season** of **rainfall**, and then move on after the rains have ended to find **water** elsewhere. Some nomads have an established pattern of moving regularly between two locations. Others move from place to place, regularly changing the site of their dwelling.

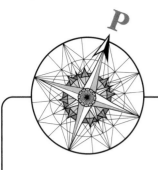

North magnetic pole

(see also **Compass** and **Polar**)

The **Earth** itself has magnetic properties. It acts like a huge magnet with two poles. At any point on the surface of the Earth, a magnetic compass will come to rest pointing in the direction of the North magnetic pole, opposite the South magnetic pole. These points are not the same as the places generally known as the North and South geographical poles.

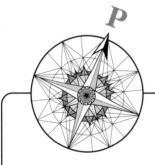

Nuclear energy

(see also **Atoms**, **Radiation** and **Energy**)

Nuclear energy is a form of energy produced by splitting atoms. If the nucleus of an atom of a substance called uranium is hit by a neutron from another atom, it will split into two parts and at the same time will release two or three neutrons of its own. This splitting is called nuclear fission. The freed neutrons can in turn cause more fission of other nuclei and produce even more neutrons . . . and so on. This continuing process is called a chain reaction.

Freed neutrons and split nuclei move at very great speed, which generates heat. This heat is the nuclear energy produced by the fission process.

Oasis

(see also **Desert**)

An oasis is an area within a desert which, unlike its barren, **arid** surroundings, is made **fertile** by the presence of **water**. An oasis may be quite a large area, some several hundred square kilometres, where desert inhabitants live and farm the land. Other oases consist of a simple stream or spring bordered by palm trees.

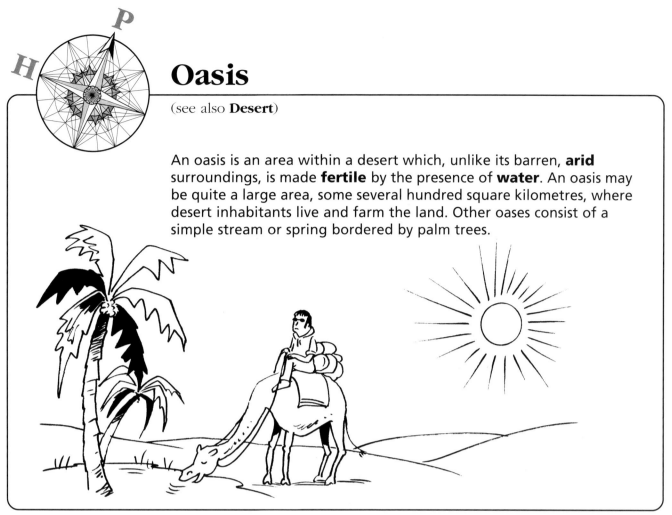

Oceans

(see also **Wetlands**)

The oceans of the world are the huge areas of salt water which surround the landmasses or **continents**. About 70% of the **Earth**'s surface is covered by oceans. The largest ocean is the Pacific, with its many small **islands**. The other major oceans are the Atlantic, the Indian, the Arctic Ocean surrounding the North Pole, and the Southern Ocean surrounding Antarctica.

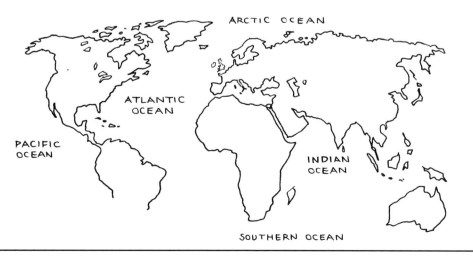

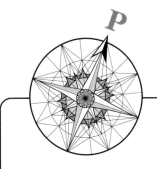

Ordnance survey

(see also **Map** and **Scale**)

The Ordnance Survey is an accurate and detailed geographical survey of the surface of Great Britain, made for the Government. The most accurate maps of Great Britain are called Ordnance Survey maps, resulting from this survey. Ordnance Survey maps are prepared by surveyors from detailed measurements. They are published in a variety of scales. Most are large scale, showing surface features in detail.

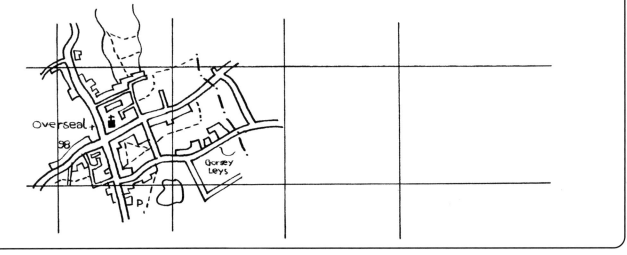

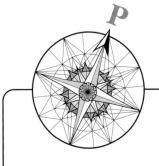

Organic fertilisers

(see also **Fertile**)

Organic fertilisers are fertilisers that are made from the remains of plants and animals, such as bones, manure and rotted plants. Sometimes they are referred to as natural fertilisers. They do not contain chemicals.

Orienteering

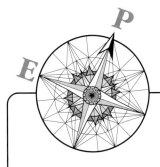

Orienteering is a sport in which competitors have to find their way across rough country, usually on foot, with the aid of a **map** and **compass**. Sometimes in snowy areas orienteering is done on cross-country skis.

Ozone layer

(see also **Global warming**)

Ozone is a gas, similar to oxygen, which occurs in the **atmosphere**. Where it occurs high up, between 15 and 55 km above the ground, it forms a protective barrier called the ozone layer that shields the **Earth** from the extreme heat of the **Sun**'s rays.

Scientists are very concerned because the ozone layer appears to be getting thinner and, in some places, developing holes. If this continues, the consequences will be disastrous. The thinning of the ozone layer is caused by **pollution** of the air by other gases.

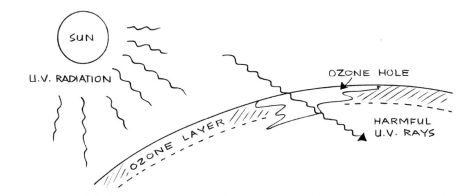

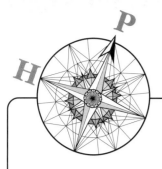

Pampas

(see also **Steppes**)

The Pampas are the mid-**latitude** grasslands that are located round the estuary of the River Plate in South America. The **region** in its wild state has a covering of natural tall grass, known as pampas grass. A good deal of the Pampas region is now used for **agriculture**. The natural grass **vegetation** has been cleared to make space for cultivating crops and rearing cattle and sheep.

Pesticides

Pesticides are chemical substances used to kill unwanted plants, insects and other small creatures. Pesticides are used by farmers to protect their crops from damage by pests. They are also sold for people to use in their homes and gardens. There is concern that pesticides cause **environmental pollution** and that they may be a danger to human **health**.

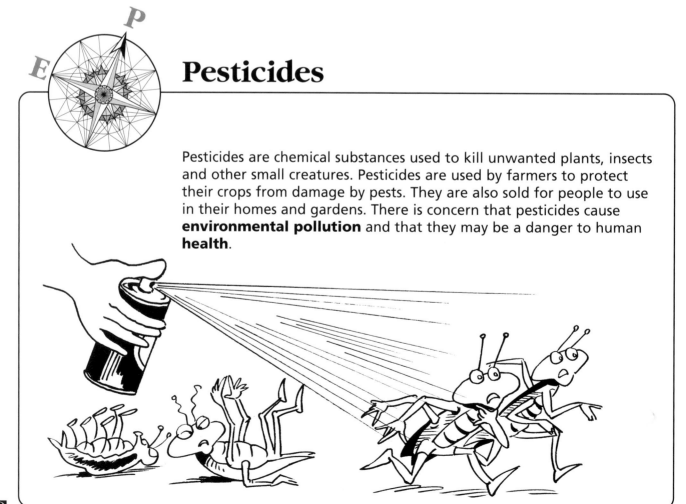

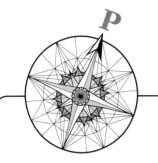

pH values

(see also **Acid rain**)

Acidity, or the amount of pH acid present in substances, is measured on a scale called a pH scale. This runs from pH 14, which is very alkaline (the opposite of acid) to pH 1, which is very acid. pH 7 at the centre of the scale is neutral. Lemon juice has a pH value of around 3, and natural **rainfall** between 5 and 6 on the scale.

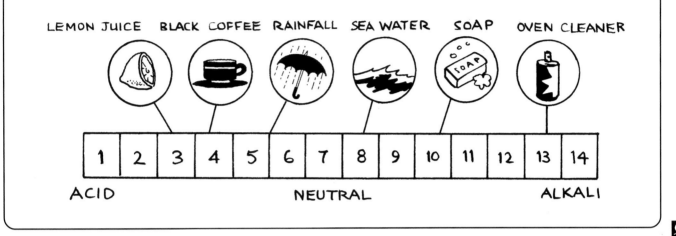

LEMON JUICE   BLACK COFFEE   RAINFALL   SEA WATER   SOAP   OVEN CLEANER

| 1 | 2 | 3 | 4 | 5 | 6 | 7 | 8 | 9 | 10 | 11 | 12 | 13 | 14 |

ACID   NEUTRAL   ALKALI

Plan

(see also **Map**)

A plan is a picture or representation of three-dimensional objects in two dimensions. Plans are the bird's eye view, or what we see from above.

Once plans are drawn, objects are fixed on paper in relation to each other.

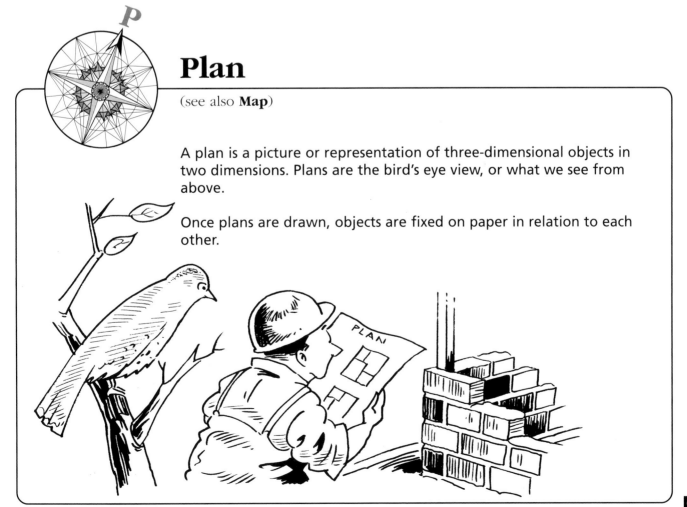

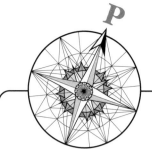

Plateau

A plateau is a large, flat area of land, which is surrounded by steep slopes and is much higher than the land that surrounds it. Some of the world's plateau areas, such as the Tibetan plateau, are higher than some ranges of **mountains**. A plateau may have **rivers** flowing across it, or even mountain ranges upon it. Some plateaux are completely enclosed by mountains. Most have an **arid climate**. Some are broken up by deep canyons or dry **valleys**.

Polar

The two points at the extreme north and south of the **Earth** are called the North and South Geographic Poles. The vast areas of land and water surrounding the Poles are very cold indeed. The area around the North Pole is known as the Arctic. It is mainly frozen **ocean**. The area surrounding the South Pole is the Antarctic. This is a huge area of land, surrounded by very cold seas. Animals, plants and people who live in the world's polar areas **adapt** to living in an **environment** characterised by ice and snow.

Pollution

Pollution means making any part of the natural world dirty, impure or unclean. **Water**, land and air may all be polluted. Pollutants, the substances that cause pollution, include smoke and gases, sewage, oil, agricultural and industrial chemicals, **radioactive** materials and many other forms of **waste**.

Population

(see also **Demography** and **Birth rates**)

The world is becoming an increasingly crowded place. The population, or number of people who live on our planet, increased rapidly in the 20th century and continues to do so. At the start of the 21st century the population is around 6,000 million.

As the number of people in the world grows, the need for resources and the amount of damage to the **environment** are also increasing.

Poverty

Millions of people in the world live in a state of poverty. They are poor. The term absolute poverty describes the state in which people live when their level of income is insufficient to provide adequate nutrition. The world's poorest people tend to live in the world's poorest and most fragile or difficult **environments**, such as **degraded** rural areas or on the edges of rapidly growing towns and cities. Poverty is a major issue in the **developing world**. In some developing nations, over half of the **population** lives in absolute poverty. Extreme poverty also exists in developed countries, especially in major cities.

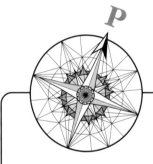

Precipitation

(see also **Rainfall** and **Hydrosphere**)

The word precipitation is used by **meteorologists** to describe all of the water, in either liquid or frozen form, which comes down to the **Earth** from the **atmosphere**. Precipitation includes rain, sleet, snow, hail, dew and frost. Often the term precipitation is used to mean the same as rainfall, that is, the total amount of water that falls on a particular place in a certain amount of time.

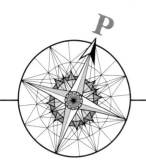

Predator

A predator is an animal that feeds upon other animals often smaller than itself. The creature hunted by the predator is called the prey. An example of a predator is a fox, which hunts prey such as hens and small wild animals.

Protected species

(see also **Species**, **Wildlife**, **Cites** and **Endangered species**)

Protected species are those species that are recognised as being endangered or likely to become endangered, and are protected in some official way. Species can be protected by law. For example, an Act of Parliament called the Wildlife and Countryside Act was passed in the United Kingdom in 1981. This Act gives various degrees of protection to all wild plants, almost all wild birds and certain wild animals. Animals specially protected by this Act include the otter, red squirrel and 15 British bats. It is a legal offence to kill, injure, take, possess or sell specially protected wildlife, and also to damage any place that they use for shelter or breeding or to disturb them when they are there.

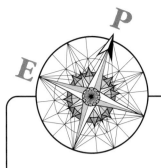

Radiation

(see also **Atoms**, **Nuclear energy** and **Hazardous waste**)

The word radiate means to spread out rays. There are many different types of radiation, including light and heat. Radiation is present all around us. To say that something is radioactive simply means that it is made up of atoms that give off rays or tiny particles of radiation at very high speed.

The air we breathe, the **Earth** we walk on, the outer space we look into and the food and drink we consume are all slightly radioactive. The small amounts of radiation in our natural **environment** and everyday life are virtually harmless. However, large doses of radiation are extremely dangerous.

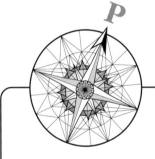

Rainfall

(see also **Precipitation**, **Clouds** and **Hydrosphere**)

Rain consists of separate drops of **water** which fall to the ground out of clouds. Rain is formed by the condensation of water vapour in the **atmosphere**.

Rainfall is the total amount of rain that falls in a particular place over a period of time. **Meteorologists** use an instrument called a rain gauge to collect and measure rainfall.

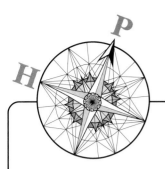

Raw materials

(see also **Renewable resources**)

Raw materials are the resources or things needed by **industry** to produce other goods or products. Examples of raw materials used by industry include iron ore, oil, timber and cotton.

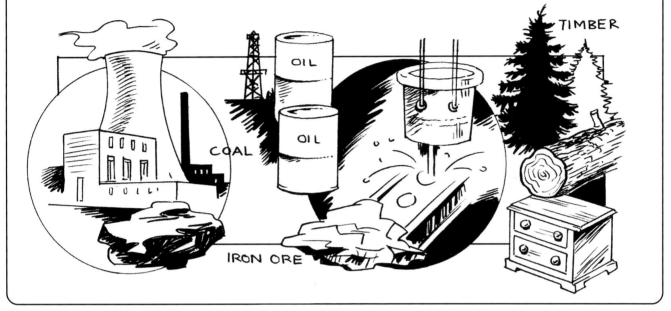

Recycling

Recycling is the conversion of **waste** into a reusable product. Items commonly recycled include bottles, paper and aluminium cans.

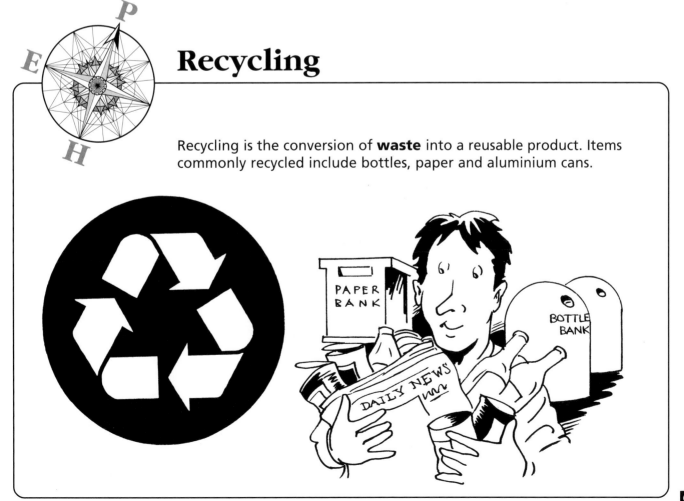

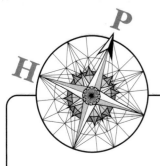

Region

(see also **Locality**)

A region is an identifiable or definable part of the world. It may be an area distinguished by natural features or by particular **climate**, **wildlife** or **vegetation**. The term may also be applied to an area of a country with its own local administration or to a group of neighbouring countries that are interdependent.

UK

WALES

NORTH WALES

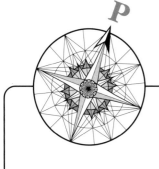

Relief

(see also **Map** and **Contour**)

Relief refers to the differences in height (elevation) of the surface of the **Earth**. A relief map shows the surface relief of a particular area. Relief models may be constructed to show surface relief in three dimensions.

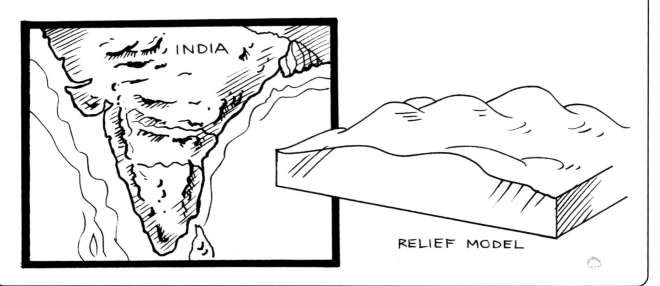

INDIA

RELIEF MODEL

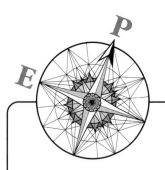

Renewable resources

Renewable resources are sources of **raw materials** or **energy** that are able to be renewed. They are not depleted or destroyed when they are used. Examples of resources, which, if properly managed where necessary, can constantly renew themselves, include food, **forest** products, water, fish, **winds**, **sun** and **tides**.

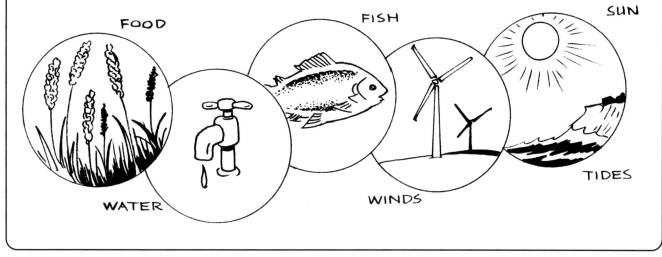

FOOD

FISH

SUN

WATER

WINDS

TIDES

Reservoir

A reservoir is a large natural or human-made **lake** or pool used for collecting and storing water for use. Usually a strong barrier called a dam is built to hold the water in the reservoir and prevent it from flooding the surrounding land.

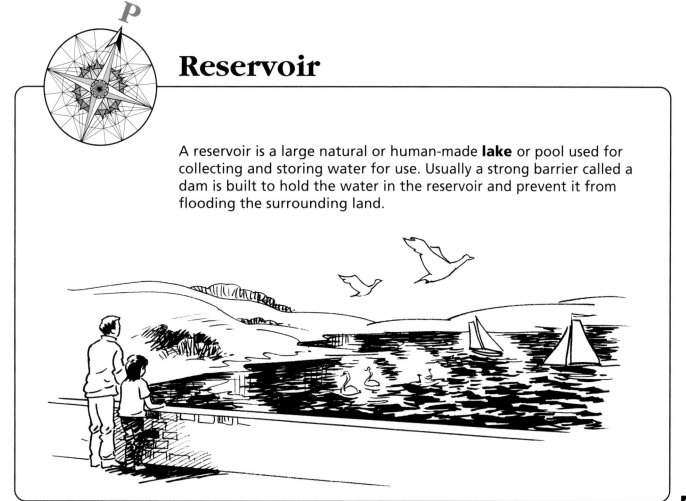

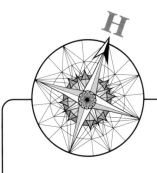

Retail industry

(see also **Industry** and **Industrialisation**)

Retail goods are items which are sold to the public in relatively small quantities and which are not for re-sale. Every time we make a purchase from a shop we are buying something retail. The 'retail industry' is a term used to describe **trade** in retail goods.

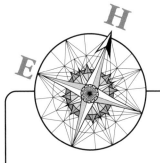

Rights

(see also **Citizenship**)

To have a right to something means to have a legitimate claim to this thing. If a human being has a right to something, then other people have a duty to make sure that the person is not prevented from getting it.

In a modern, fair and just society, all citizens should be equal in terms of how they are treated. Every person should be entitled to a variety of 'rights' or expectations of treatment and opportunities that are automatic. Rights include civil rights, political rights, social rights and human rights. Rights can be violated by various forms of injustice, **inequality** and discrimination including racism and sexism.

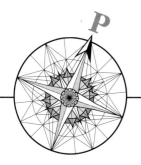

River

Fresh water flowing along a natural channel in the ground is called a river. Smaller streams, brooks and tributaries flow into a main river. The flowing water is confined within riverbanks. A river flows into the sea, a **lake** or into another river.

A river originates at a place known as its source that may be a spring, a lake or a small stream. The **route** followed by a river is called its course.

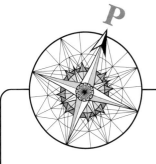

Rock

(see also **Lithosphere** and **Minerals**)

Rock is the solid material that forms the crust of the **Earth** in the lithoshpere. Rock is made up of minerals, but it does not have a definite chemical composition as minerals do. There are many different types of rock. Geologists, who study the materials of which the Earth is made, have divided rocks into three major groups or classes: sedimentary rocks, igneous rocks and metamorphic rocks.

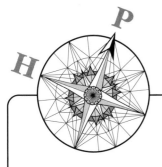

Route

A route is a way, a road or a course of travel for getting from one place to another. **Maps** show routes such as footpaths, roads and railways. Some long distance routes are travelled regularly for the purposes of **trade**.

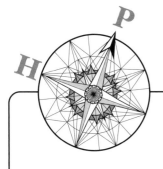

Satellite image

A satellite is a machine in space orbit around the **Earth**. Pictures or images of the surface of our planet can be taken from satellites and transmitted back to Earth.

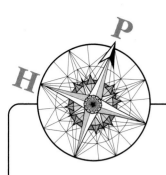

Scale

A scale is the ratio between the distance between two points on a **map** and the actual distance it represents. A scale may be expressed by the two lengths, for example, 4 cm to 1 km. A scale of this ratio would be used for what is called a large-scale map, where the lengths on the map representing actual distances are quite large. Most **ordnance survey** maps are large scale. They show **landscape** features in great detail. On small-scale maps, the lengths representing actual distances are smaller, so the features cannot be shown in as much detail.

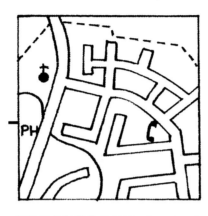

Sea level

(see also **Contour**)

The term sea level is used to refer to the level that the surface of the sea would lie at if it were not affected by **tides** or waves. Mean Sea Level is the mean (average) level between high and low tide in a place. This is the standard level from which heights of land above the sea are calculated.

5m ABOVE SEA LEVEL

SEA LEVEL

Seasons

P

Seasons are periods of the year which are characterised by particular aspects of **climate** and changes in **vegetation**. In **temperate regions** there are four **seasons**, each lasting three months. In the northern **hemisphere** the seasons are: Spring (March, April, May); Summer (June, July, August); Autumn (September, October, November) and Winter (December, January, February). In the southern hemisphere, the seasonal months are the opposite of these. Spring is September, October, November and so on.

NORTHERN HEMISPHERE	SPRING	SUMMER	AUTUMN	WINTER
SOUTHERN HEMISPHERE	AUTUMN	WINTER	SPRING	SUMMER

Settlements

H

A settlement is the term used to describe a small village or collection of houses, especially in a remote place. It is also used to refer to a place where immigrants or colonists have made their home in a new country.

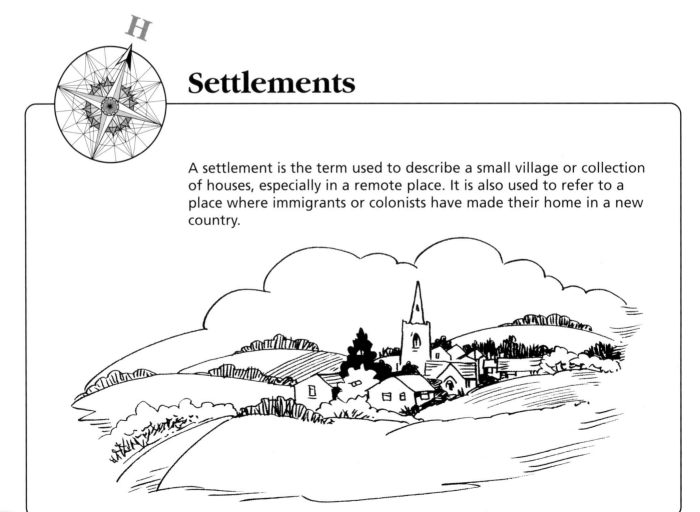

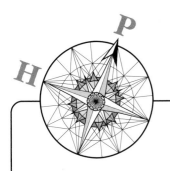

Slash and burn

Slash and burn is a traditional method of farming in which an area of land is cleared by the cutting of trees and bushes, and is then burned. When the **soil** is exhausted (i.e. no longer capable of supporting plant life), another area in the **forest** is cleared in this way.

Soil

Soil is the loose material that forms the upper layer of the **lithosphere** and lies on the **rock** of the **Earth**'s crust. Soil is made up of very small particles. It may have a depth of only a fraction of a centimetre, or of several metres. Soil is mainly comprised of **mineral** material, which has broken away from rock through the process of **weathering**. It also contains humus, which is decomposed or partly decomposed organic matter deriving from dead animal and plant life. Water and air fill the spaces between the solid soil particles. Scientists divide the world's soils into various groups according to their characteristics and materials from which they are made.

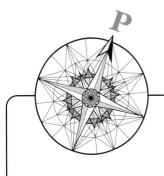

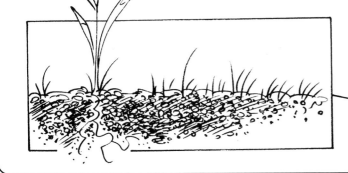

ROCK

LITHOSPHERE

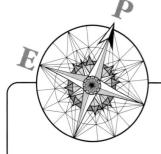

Solar system

(see also **Sun** and **Universe**)

The term solar system refers to a group of celestial bodies. It includes the Sun, the nine large planets that revolve around the Sun, smaller planets or Asteroids, Comets, Meteors and Meteorites. The solar system also includes the satellites that revolve around the planets, for example, the Moon that moves round planet **Earth**. It does not include the stars, which are actually other suns lying at huge distances from the Earth.

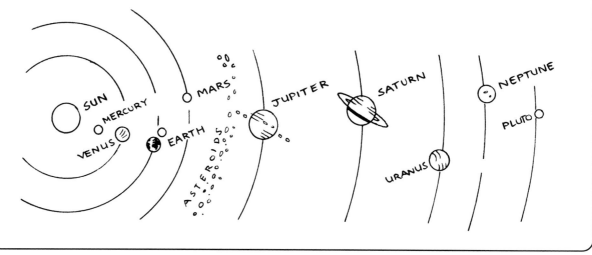

Species

(see also **Endangered species**)

A species is a particular type or family of living thing, which shares similar characteristics with other members of the same species. There are over 13,000 known species of mammals and birds in our world, thousands of species of reptiles and fish, some 250,000 species of plants, and millions of invertebrates.

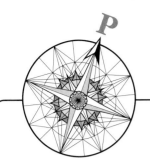

Stalactites and stalagmites

(see also **Cave** and **Minerals**)

Stalactites and stalagmites are columns of minerals found in underground caves. Stalactites, usually formed of calcium carbonate, hang like icicles from the cave roof. Stalagmites, again made of calcium carbonate, form columns which project upwards from the floor. Stalagmites are often made from water containing dissolved calcium carbonate, which drips down from stalactites. Sometimes stalactites and stalagmites meet as they develop and form a continuous pillar that joins the floor and the roof of a cave.

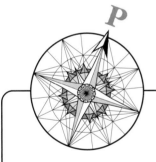

Steppes

(see also **Pampas**)

Steppes are large areas of land where grasses grow naturally. These grasslands are in **regions** of mid-**latitude**, that is, mid-way between the **equator** and **polar** areas. The word Steppes is usually used to describe the grassy plains found in some regions of Europe. Other words are used to describe similar treeless plains in other **continents**, for example, Prairies in North America and Pampas in South America

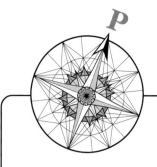

Stevenson screen

(see also **Meteorology** and **Weather**)

A Stevenson screen is the name given to the standard container or shelter used by meteorologists for some of their instruments.

A Stevenson screen is a white wooden box, raised up above the ground. It usually contains thermometers for measuring **temperature** and instruments for measuring humidity. The screen is designed so that air can freely circulate in and out of it through gaps in its wooden frame.

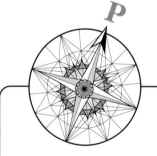

Sun

(see also **Universe** and **Solar system**)

The Sun is the enormous star at the centre of our solar system. It is a gigantic ball of burning gas, which has nine planets in orbit around it.

The Sun is crucial to life on **Earth**. It provides both light and heat, and its force of gravity keeps the Earth in its position.

The diameter of the Sun is around 100 times greater than that of the Earth. It is estimated that the Sun will survive for a further 5,000 million years.

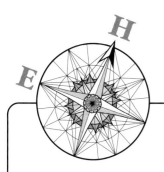

Sustainable development

(see also **Development**)

Sustainable development is the term used to refer to a very great challenge facing the people of the world today – that is, continuing to make progress (development) in society, and at the same time, making sure that the **environment** and its resources are protected. Sustainable development involves developments which meet the needs of people alive on **Earth** today *without* destroying or degrading the environment and its resources which will be needed by people of the future.

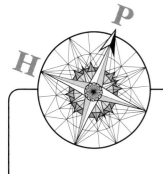

Symbols

(see also **Key**)

Symbols are small pictures, diagrams or marks that represent real objects or **landscape** features on a **map** or **plan**.

Technology

Technology is the aspect of knowledge that deals with mechanical matters, or applied sciences such as electronics. At the present time we are said to live in a high technology society, that is, a world with advanced technological equipment, especially in electronics. New technology is technology that radically alters the way in which something is produced or done, such as automation or computerisation.

Temperate

(see also **Latitude**)

The temperate **regions** of the world are those which lie in the middle latitudes, that is, the zones between the Tropic of Cancer and the Arctic Circle in the Northern **hemisphere**, and between the Tropic of Capricorn and the Antarctic Circle in the Southern hemisphere. In these areas, unlike the **tropics**, the **Sun** is never directly overhead. In temperate regions these are distinct **seasons** of the year.

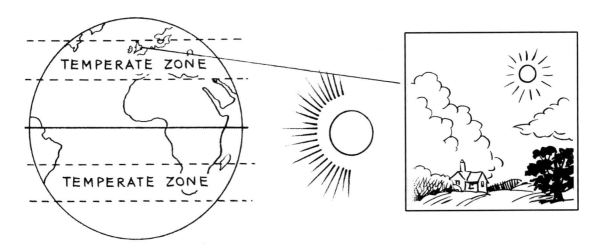

Temperature

Temperature is a measure of the hotness or degree of heat of something. Usually temperature is expressed as degrees on a Centigrade Scale or a Fahrenheit Scale. Meteorologists measure the temperature of the air using instruments called thermometers.

Places with the highest temperatures on **Earth** are near to the **equator**. Generally, temperatures decrease with distance from the equator towards the North and South Poles.

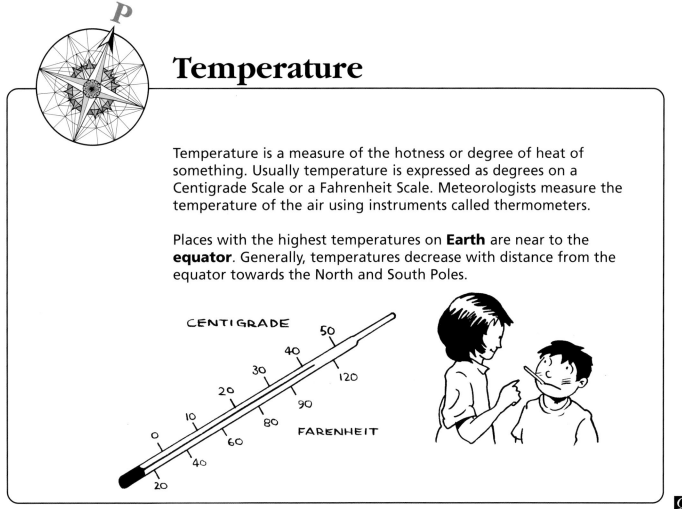

Tides

Approximately twice a day the surface of the world's **oceans** and seas rises and falls. This regular movement is called tides. Tides occur because of force of gravity. The Moon in particular, and to a lesser extent the **Sun**, have a 'pull' of gravity which affects the **Earth**'s large surfaces of water. Tides may be regarded as two very large waves affecting the water's surface. Far out to sea they would hardly be noticed, but near to the edges of **continents** the difference between the level of the sea at high tide and the level at low tide may be significant. We notice the effects of tides at the seashore. When the tide is high or in, more of the beach will be covered with water than when it is low or out.

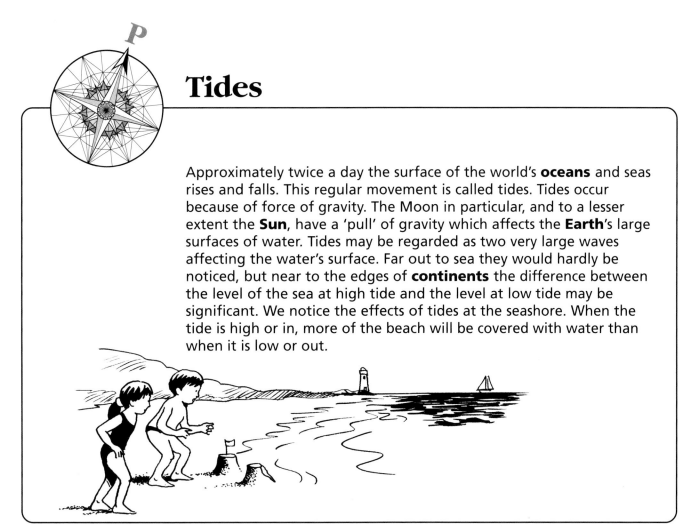

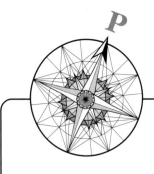

Topography

Topography is a detailed description or representation of **landforms** and **landscape** features. A topographic **map** is a large-scale map showing these features in detail. A topographic map is likely to show **relief** with **contours** and other features such as roads, paths, railways, streams, **rivers** and **lakes**.

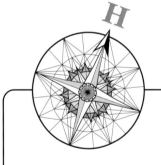

Trade

(see also **Imports and exports**)

Trade is the exchange of goods and other services for economic benefit.

Items may be traded between individuals or businesses within a country, or between countries. Railways, roads, **rivers** and canals serve as important over-land trade **routes**. Cargo ships carry imports and exports across the **oceans**, and aeroplanes convey light goods, mail and passengers across the trade routes of the sky.

Transport

To transport means to convey people or goods by land, sea or air. Forms of transport include bicycle, car, truck, train, hovercraft, ferry, tanker, barge, ocean liner and jet aircraft. Transport moves along transportation **routes**, which include roads, railway lines, canals, and agreed shipping and air routes.

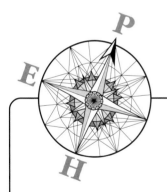

Tropical rainforests

(see also **Tropics**, **Deforestation** and **Biodiversity**)

Some parts of planet **Earth** are covered with vast areas of evergreen **forest** land that receive vary large amounts of **rainfall**. These places are known as tropical rainforests. They lie in the tropics, north and south of the **equator**, where the **climate** is generally hot and wet. Originally the area of the world covered by these forests was much larger than it is today.

CANOPY

FOREST FLOOR

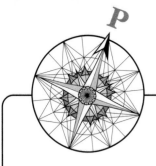

Tropics

(see also **Tropicalrain forests**)

The tropics is a term generally used to describe **regions** of the world that lie between two particular lines of **latitude**, namely the Tropic of Cancer and the Tropic of Capricorn. The Tropic of Cancer lies about 23° north of the **equator** and the Tropic of Capricorn the same distance south of the equator. The region between these lines of latitude has a tropical **climate**, with very hot **temperature**. The **Sun** is almost directly overhead a good deal of the time.

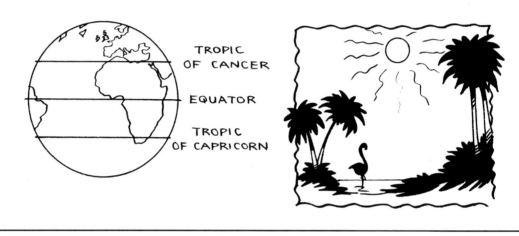

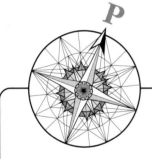

Tsunami

(see also **Earthquake**)

A tsunami is a very large wave that sometimes occurs along the **coasts** of Japan and other locations, particularly in the Pacific Ocean. The tsunami is caused when an earthquake occurs at the floor of the **ocean**. As the wave gets nearer to the coastline it grows higher and higher until it eventually breaks on to the land with massive force. The tsunami can cause great damage and has been known to drown many people.

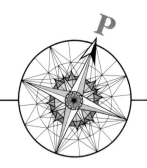

Tundra

The Tundra is the **region** of the world in the northern **hemisphere** consisting of the treeless plains of North America and northern Europe and Asia. For most of the year, **temperatures** in the Tundra are below freezing point. Winters are long and extremely cold. Snow covers the ground for most of the year. The short summers are warmer, but even then, the ground just below the surface remains frozen. Mosses and lichens appear on the ground in summer months, but no trees are able to grow in the Tundra regions.

UNCED

United Nations' Conference on Environment and Development.

In June 1992 the United Nations organisation held a major international conference on Environment and Development in Rio de Janeiro, Brazil. Sometimes this event is referred to as the Earth Summit. Around 10,000 people attended the conference from 150 countries. UNCED produced five major documents, which included two international agreements on **environmental** issues, two statements of principles relating to environment and **development**, and a major action agenda (**Agenda 21**) on world-wide **sustainable development**.

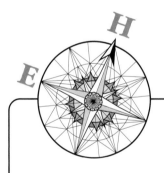

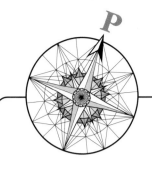

Universe

(see also **Solar system** and **Sun**)

The universe is the term used for the whole of space as we know it. It is made up of millions of collections of stars called galaxies. The galaxy in which we live is called the Milky Way, which has around 250,000,000,000 stars. One huge star in the Milky Way is the Sun, and the **Earth** is one of the nine planets that move around the Sun.

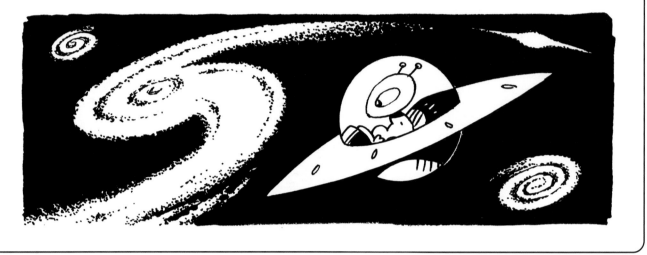

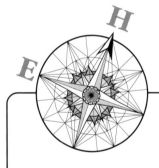

Urbanisation

Urbanisation is the process of growth or **development** of towns and cities, and the gradual movement of many of the world's people into an urban or built **environment**. The proportion of the world's people living in urban areas is rising. At the present time it is around half of the total **population**.

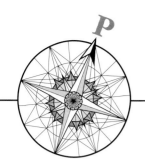

Valley

A valley is a long, narrow depression in the surface of the **Earth**, with sides sloping downwards to its bottom or valley floor. Streams and **rivers** flow through valleys. Their water carves out the valley from the **rocks** through the process of **erosion**. Valleys vary greatly in size and shape. They may be narrow with steep sides, shaped like the letter V or they may be much wider with more gently sloping sides. **Glaciers** also carve valleys as they move across rocks. A glacial valley is shaped like the letter U.

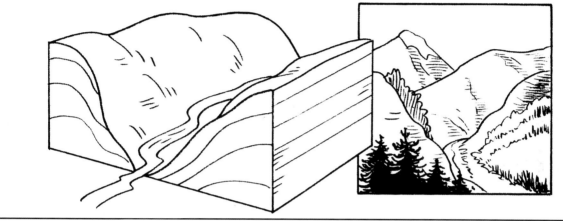

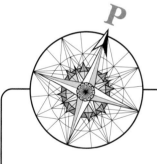

Vegetation

Vegetation means plant cover or growth in a particular location. The term natural vegetation refers to the plants that would normally grow on and dominate an area or **habitat**.

Volcano

(see also **Natural hazards**)

A volcano is a vent or gap in the crust of the **Earth**. It is formed when molten material (magma), which usually exists below the solid **rock** of the crust, forces its way upward to the surface. This molten rock or lava may shoot out of the volcano with great force. When this happens, it is called an eruption. Volcanic eruptions can cause tremendous damage. Extremely hot liquid lava, gases and pieces of solid magma pour out on to the surrounding land. Volcanoes are usually shaped like conical **mountains**. Their sides are built up of material which has been poured out in eruptions over thousands of years.

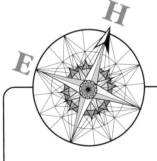

War and conflict

War is a state of armed hostility or conflict between opposing groups of people. Wars often take place between two or more countries because they have disagreement over ownership of land. Wars may cause serious **degradation** and damage to the **environment**.

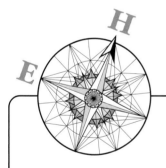

Waste

(see also **Hazardous waste** and **Recycling**)

The word waste means something that is left over after use, superfluous, and no longer serving a purpose. For a long time, people have been generally in the habit of throwing away such materials, believing that they no longer have value and cannot be put to further use.

WCED

The *World Commission on Environment and Development* (WCED) was established in 1983, and was chaired by the person who was Prime Minister of Norway at that time, Mrs. Gro Harlem Brundtland. The Commission, which included individuals from 22 nations, produced the first major international report on **environment** and **development** issues, known as the **Brundtland report**.

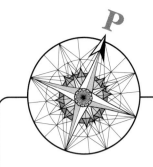

Weather

(see also **Stevenson screen** and **Meteorology**)

Weather describes the particular condition of the **atmosphere** at a certain time or over a short period of time. This description includes details of atmospheric pressure, **temperature**, humidity, **rainfall**, **clouds**, **wind** speed and wind direction. Detailed observations, readings or measurements of these phenomena are taken with appropriate scientific instruments. Details relating to the weather are plotted on charts and **maps**. It is possible to predict or forecast the weather by studying these charts. A weather chart is known as a synoptic chart because it presents a synopsis of the meteorological situation at a particular time.

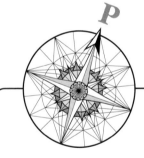

Weathering

(see also **Acid rain**)

Weathering describes the breaking down or gradual disintegration of the **rocks** of the **Earth**, **landforms** and buildings as a result of long term exposure to the **atmosphere**. The process of weathering may be either chemical or mechanical. An example of chemical weathering is acid rain, when the acidic chemicals in rain water gradually dissolve and break down limestone rock. Rain, wind, **Sun** and ice all contribute to mechanical weathering. For example, the heat of the Sun causes rocks to expand. Subsequent cooling causes them to contract. In time, this continual alternate expansion and contraction causes rocks to crack and break up.

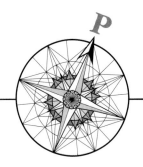

Well

A well is a place where underground water is made accessible at the surface of the ground. A hole has been drilled or dug from the ground down to the place where water lies. The water can be pumped or raised up to the surface in a container.

The term, well, is also used in connection with access to supplies of oil that lie below the surface of the ground or seabed.

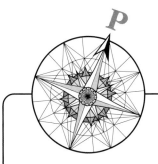

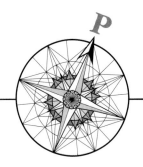

Wetlands

(see also **Fresh water** and **Oceans**)

Wetlands is the name given to all areas other than oceans that are permanently or periodically covered in water. Wetlands include areas of marsh, fen, peatland, bogand water. They may be natural or artificial, permanent or temporary. The water may be still or flowing. Wetlands include seawater where it is less than six metres deep, and all **rivers** and water adjacent to **coasts**.

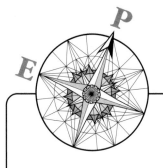

Wilderness

A wilderness is a natural **habitat** that has had little or no disturbance from the activities of people. A wilderness is wild, uncultivated and inhabited only by wild creatures.

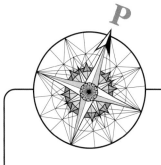

Wildlife

(see also **Protected species** and **Endangered species**)

Wildlife is a term generally used to describe all forms of animal life (mammals, birds, amphibians, reptiles, fish and invertebrates) which live in natural **habitats**.

Wind

(see also **Beaufort scale**)

A wind is a current of air, moving in any direction. The direction of a wind is identified by the point of the **compass** from which it is blowing. So, for example, a north wind blows from the north. Meteorologists measure the speed that a wind is blowing and its velocity. A wind that blows frequently from the same direction in any particular place is called a prevailing wind. Certain winds blow regularly across parts of the **Earth**'s surface and are known as planetary winds.

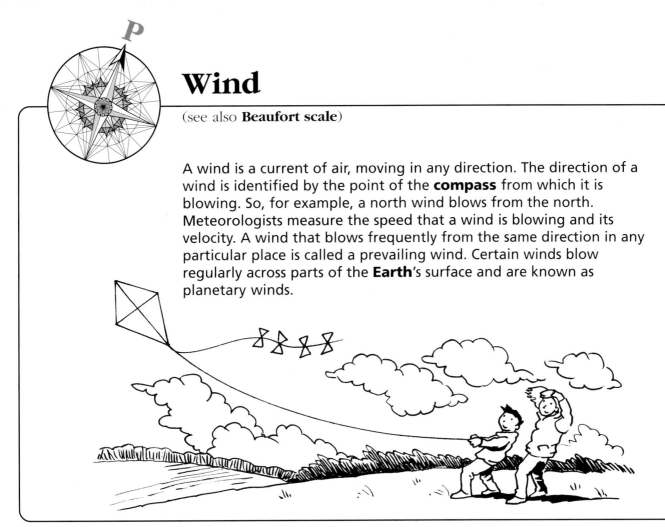

Women and the environment

Women may have a key role to play in encouraging **sustainable development** in the **developing world**. In many areas in developing countries, it is the women who grow food and manage **agriculture**, who collect the household's water and who are responsible for **wood** supplies and **energy** resources. Where there is **soil erosion**, drought and **deforestation**, it is the women who largely suffer the difficulties of maintaining their activities. They depend on a healthy **environment**. They understand the importance of environmental protection.

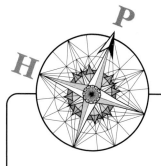

Wood

(see also **Forests**)

A wood is a group of trees which may be relatively small, or big enough to be described as a small forest.

The word wood, is also used to describe the timber derived from the trees. Timber varies greatly in its qualities. Some trees provide much stronger, harder wood than others. Some varieties of wood are better suited to making such things as paper and small items. Other varieties are better suited for more substantial things such a ships and buildings.

© Questions Publishing Limited

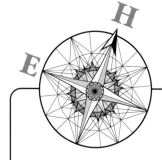

World Bank

The World Bank, or the International Bank for Reconstruction and Development, is the major source of funds for the **developing world**. If the World Bank agrees to put money into a **development** project, then other banks, agencies and governments will contribute also. The main objectives of the World Bank are reducing **poverty** and promoting **sustainable development**. The World Bank lends money to individual governments for specific projects.

© Questions Publishing Limited